THE BRAVE WAY

Shadow River Ink
Box 222
Rosseau, ON   P0C 1J0
www.shadowriver.ca

Ordering Information:
Available from bravewomen.ca. Quantity sales: Special discounts may be available on quantity purchases by corporations, educational institutions, and others. For details, contact the publisher at the address above.

Orders by trade bookstores and wholesalers. Please contact Ingram:
North America - Tel: (800) 937-0152
All other areas - Tel: (615) 213-5000
or visit www.ingramcontent.com

Printed in the United States of America

Publisher's Cataloging-in-Publication data
Duffield, Ellen.
The brave way : where will your brave take you today? / by Ellen Duffield.
226 p. 21.6 x 21.6 cm.
ISBN
1. Leadership. 2. Leadership in women. 3. Social action. 4. Social change. I. Duffield, Ellen.

First Edition
22 21 20 19 18 / 10 9 8 7 6 5 4 3 2 1

Cover and Interior Design: Shadow River Ink
Cover Photo: Brooke Cagle. @brookecagle / Unsplash.com

Special thanks to: Tim Duffield, Sheila Webster, Carrie Fleetwood, M.Ed, OACCPP, R.P.

THE BRAVE WAY

Where will your BRAVE take you today?

BY ELLEN DUFFIELD

SHADOW RIVER INK
An Independent Publisher

shadowriver.ca

Life is an epic journey. To live it well we must find our way… our Brave way…to where we belong, to our true selves and to our true calling.

Our world needs us, and some things are worth fighting for.

BRAVE

When Auntie Lilas came to visit we had to be on our best behaviour. She noticed every speck of dirt or breach of table etiquette. I was afraid of her... and yet I adored her. Growing up in a house where dinner out meant take out chips, Aunt Lilas introduced me to restaurants with white tablecloths and rows of shiny silver. She took me to my first ballet and gave me age inappropriate gifts like art and poetry books when I was four.

One of these books I still have. I keep it wrapped in tissue as the leather cover disintegrates when touched. It is the poetry of Pauline Johnson. Because of Aunt Lilas, Pauline has been a hero of mine since I was perhaps 5 years old. Emily Pauline Johnson was born in 1861. The year Abraham Lincoln became President of the United States. She was the youngest of four children born to a Mohawk chief father and English mother.

Her Mohawk name was *Tekahionwake*–pronounced: dageh-eeon-wageh, which meant literally, "two lives." When speaking in England, Pauline advocated for the important causes her Mohawk community espoused.*

Like many BRAVE leaders Pauline was not always well received. Booed off stages, criticized in the press and dismissed by many friends and family members she carried on, travelling across Canada and the United Kingdom to speak and write.

Pauline demonstrates many of the attributes of a BRAVE Leader.

She was Brave.

She was Resilient.

She was an Advocate and Activist.

She discovered and used her Voice.

She Expanded her view of the world and helped others to do the same.

You can imagine how excited I was when, moving to Muskoka, I discovered that she had often camped along the shoreline on our lake! In fact one of my favorite of Pauline's poems, "Shadow River," was written about the stream two kilometers from our home. In this poem Pauline reflects on how still the water is. Canoeing the river I have often noticed the mirror like surface of the water and incredible scenery. It is stunningly beautiful.

Pauline realized that dipping her paddle to move forward would ripple the water and distort the reflection. Her poem effortlessly weaves Pauline's deep love for nature and her desire for peace with her willingness to make waves if necessary. As a poet, lecturer, speaker, and advocate for the environment, peace, and

*These included protecting the environment (at a time when England was exploding with factories that were raping the land with destructive practices and pollution as well as forcing small, undernourished children to work long hours in unhealthy environments); equality amongst people groups (at a time when this was anything but the case); and equality for women (at a time when Suffragettes were lobbying for votes for women but women in traditional Mohawk societies were respected leaders).

Reflect: Who are the heroes who have shaped your worldview? Who invites you to believe and speak and act?

equality she truly was a woman before her time. From an early age, I was fascinated by the power of her passion and only later understood how difficult it must have been for a young woman at that time to find and use her voice so bravely.

Looking objectively at our world we see that we are in need of many Paulines. BRAVE people who refuse to let mixed messages, fears and perceptions impact our beliefs about power and courage. People who refuse to take the obvious, easier paths of pride, or self-demeaning. People who choose the harder but so much more life giving BRAVE path.

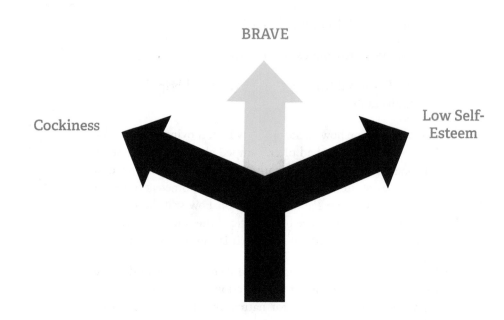

12

To LIVE FULLY INTO OUR EPIC STORY TAKES COURAGE. Yet, low self-confidence debilitates many of us before we even begin. Ironically, the people who we think least likely to struggle with low-confidence, are often struggling the most.

We need to find our footing again.

We need to rediscover who we are and what is possible when we band together in radical friendships and set out to change our world.

This book will take us on just such a shared journey. Before we start, we may need a new set of lenses through which to view our world and ourselves. Or more accurately a new set of shoes—maybe even three pairs. A pair of yellow flip flops for fun, a pair of sneakers for traction, and perhaps a pair of yellow heels to take us down some corridors.

Why yellow? Yellow is a bright, fun colour that doesn't take itself too seriously. Even more importantly, it has traditionally been associated with cowardice. It is time to redeem yellow to mean true Bravery.

Why footwear? Low confidence stops us from jumping in. Footwear suggests movement but allows that movement to be at our own pace. We can tiptoe, stroll, dance, advance our wheelchair, run, skip or jump and still make a profound difference in our world.

Why travel together? Friendships are important, and if we want to see the kind of global changes we are longing to see, we will not be able to do that alone. As Margaret Mead once said:

"Never doubt that a small group of thoughtful, committed citizens can change the world; indeed, it is the only thing that ever has."

The journey will take us to some wild places, starting with the dirt beneath our feet!

Dirt is amazing. Not the urban dust that blackens the air or the potting soil in heat-sealed plastic but the rich, black humus found in ancient stands of forest or under bogs and wetlands. A single cupful of that kind of soil may contain as many bacteria as there are people on the earth. A single shovelful may contain more species than live in the entire Amazon forest. Filled with carbon, nitrogen, oxygen, potassium, and magnesium from rotting organic material, and minerals from weathering rocks, humus is a truly diverse community of living and non-living things.

This is the kind of dirt that life springs from. Towering redwoods. Tiny tendrils. Not to mention the cocoa and coffee that some days seem crucial to life. Did you know that "scientists have identified as many as fifteen-hundred distinct chemical compounds in the coffee bean?"[1] What a gloriously complex world we live in! And human beings are much more complex than a single coffee bean. In fact, the more I think about human transformation the more I am brought back to the simplicity and complexity of dirt.

The word human comes from the same root word as humus, which is apt since we also are made of oxygen, carbon, hydrogen, nitrogen, and other elements found in the rich brown-black earth of the forest floor. We are a people rooted in the grittiest, most trod-upon, spit-out, brushed-off and yet wonder-filled of substances. Dirt.

The mud on our sneakers contains the same elements as a newborn baby or a granny in her rocker on the front porch.

A chemist might add that we are also made of water since 65% of the trillions of cells and millions of bacteria that make up our physical bodies are H_2O. We are the stuff of seas, salt tears, and spring water bubbling up from the ground in unexpected places.

A physicist might argue that we are actually made of nothing since 99.9% of any atom is empty space. Someone has calculated that if we could remove all the empty space in our atoms, the entire human population would fit into an area the size of a sugar cube! We are the stuff of mystery.

Why don't we implode? You may recall from science class that electrons and nuclei repel each other, creating orbits so big that if a nucleus were the size of a bean sitting on a pitcher's mound, the electrons would be travelling around the outside of the diamond. These same electromagnetic forces enable us to see a sunset, laugh at a joke, scratch our nose, run a marathon or dance the salsa. Amazingly, the same force also brings us starlight travelling at the speed of light. We are the stuff of stars.

Barely aware of the thought processes involved, we open our mouths and sounds that carry insight or longing come out and are understood (or not) by others.

We take a deep breath, and the breezes of the Himalayas enter our lungs and transfer oxygen through 60,000 miles of our blood vessels.

What amazing beings we are! The stuff of stars, and seas, and soil. We are breathing air that may have circumnavigated the globe and balancing complex interactive systems just to hold and read this book.

Yet we look in a mirror and notice only the flaws.

Humus and human share their Latin root with yet another word, humility, meaning to be grounded or from the earth. Now that we know how vibrantly diverse and teeming with life humus is, we can better appreciate the original meaning. To be humble was not understood by the ancients as having a low self-image or being used—just the opposite. To be humble meant to stand in amazement at how complex and valuable we are, while at the same time being equally amazed at everyone and everything else! It meant embracing a sense of wonder. Remaining open and curious. To enjoy and let others enjoy. To live fully. To celebrate.

Humility was also understood as a relational term involving deep respect for self and others partnered with genuine compassion for our own and others' weaknesses.

As 12th C Hildegard of Bingen wrote,

"[True] humility does not rob people or take anything from [us]. Rather it holds together everything in love."

True humility values both the self and others as beautiful *and* imperfect beings. It enables the genuine comradeship that fuels our desire to assist others on their journey, as they accompany us on ours.

Humility is a fundamental appreciation of what it means to be human. Destiny clothed in the dirt. Mystery mixed with the mundane. Esteem embracing empathy. No wonder the highest form of humility was—and still is—expressed in the service of others.

And no wonder that, understood correctly, the more truly humble we are, the more confident, healthy and happy we will be.

BRAVE, as we are defining it here, is not cockiness or even feeling good about ourselves. It is about doing the right thing: speaking up for what we believe in, stepping outside our comfort zone to make our world a better place, even when it feels down right scary, and even when there may be a cost.

Bravery is not the opposite of fear. Nor is it a false bravado, aggressiveness, the denial of genuine emotion or lack of thoughtful hesitation. It is not a reckless risk-taking that comes at the expense of our selves or others.

Bravery is a choice. It is the moment-by-moment victory that occurs when we are afraid but act anyway. It is about becoming at home in our own skin and with our own voice. It is what happens when we allow ourselves to notice what we have carefully kept ourselves from seeing. BRAVE is what happens when speaking up or taking action becomes the only option imaginable to us. At the risk of sounding like a Hallmark card; it is what happens when hope replaces fear. It is what happens when we dare to love.

For the opposite of fear is love—of someone or something important to you. For you, it could be nature, beauty, fairness, humanity, faith, equality, freedom, or truth. Sometimes it is a love for people sitting in the audience you are about to address.

BRAVE is an acronym to help us remember: the Bravery this will take; the Resiliency it will require; the skills of Advocacy and Action we can use; the Voice every one of us can find; and the Expanding Perspective that will enable us to increase our influence in this amazing yet still flawed world in which we have the incredible privilege to live.

B old, Balanced, Beautiful, and Bright
R esilient
A dvocates and Activists
V oice
E xpanded Perspective and Influence

I remember the first time I thought seriously about bravery. Caught between a much older boy flicking a wet towel at my bare legs and a locked school door at the tender age of five I learned that bravery often confronts a bully. It was not until later that I realized that sometimes the bully that would show up would be within me—an inner voice telling me either that I was not enough or that I was too much. Sometimes the bully even shows up in the voices and actions of our dearest friends and family members. Perhaps without them even knowing it. There is often a relational or personal cost to true bravery.

Perhaps that is one of the reasons why so many women and girls are drowning in a sea of low confidence. The personal, organizational and community costs are staggering. Low self-esteem has been linked to violent behaviour, school dropout rates, teenage pregnancy, suicide, and low academic achievement.[2] Low self confidence leads to indecision and inaction, while opportunity plus confidence enables dramatic positive influence.

We know that empowering women translates into community transformation. As early as the 1990s, the United Nations and the World Bank began to appreciate the potential resource that women and girls represent. UNICEF issued a major report arguing that gender equality yields a "double dividend" by elevating not only women but also their children and communities. The Hunger Project proclaims, "Women are key to ending hunger in Africa."

Doctors Without Borders asserts, "Progress is achieved through women."[3]

Many microenterprises have discovered that when loans are made to women, they are not only much more likely to be repaid but also to cause ripple effect like improvements in the whole community as women, now empowered by cottage industries, begin to address the social needs around them.[4] Schools, clean water, health care facilities and other positive initiatives are much more likely to emerge.

19

When women are included in peacekeeping negotiations levels of conflict go down. Balanced business teams are more successful on every front. Having women in local and national decision-making roles increases financial stability, creates healthier and more humane cultures, and reduces crime and corruption. Some security experts note that countries that nurture terrorists "are disproportionately those where women are marginalized."[5]

Over two decades ago Rosabeth Moss Kanter discovered that we need a minimum of 30% women on a leadership team in order to see the benefits of a balanced team. Any less than this and most women will not feel like they can "show up as themselves" and teams will not have the balanced influence needed to make wiser decisions. Many studies since have validated this finding. For example, several studies have found that women speak less than men in meetings where both are present. One Princeton University research team found that, in some cases, when women were in the minority, they spoke 75% less than the men did.[6]

The importance of 30% to create well-balanced teams is such a well-established norm that in the year 2000 189 countries optimistically agreed to UN set Millennial Goals to empower women to raise the quality of life in communities globally. Huge resources were put towards the effort. Yet few of these goals have been reached. While the reasons for this are complex, one thing is clear: this is more challenging than we first thought.

It is going to take thousands upon thousands of us to bridge this gap. For currently, girls and women are under-represented as leaders and overrepresented as victims of injustice around the world.

More girls are killed in routine "gendercide in any one decade than people have been slaughtered in all genocides of the 20th C"—aborted because of their gender, killed in domestic violence or honor killings, dying from complications from female genital mutilation, etc.[7]

While precise figures are difficult to determine, it is believed that up to 80% of the 30+ million people held as slaves today are girls and women.[8]

According to the UN, women are more likely to live in poverty than men.[9] In fact, women produce 2/3's of the world's work hours but earn 1/10th of its income.[10] Girls and women spend 90% of their earned income on their family while men spend 30-40%.[11]

Two-thirds of the world's illiterate are women.[12] While the situation is improving, girls have equal access to education in only 40% of the world.[13]

The UN Food and Agriculture Organization reports that in developing countries, only 10-20% of all landowners are women, but they make up 43% of the agricultural workforce.[14]

Elderly women in the US are twice as likely to live in poverty as their male peers.[15]

However, where women and men are serving together there are encouraging signs of community change.

Reflect: What social justice issues are important to you? How might they be resolved more quickly if women and men partnered as BRAVE leaders?

Sadly, our fundamental needs to truly belong, to fully be ourselves and to bring something meaningful to the table have been undermined by internal and external forces that rob us of the joy of confidently embracing the journey. To be joyfully ourselves, to own our flaws and to embrace our strengths; to welcome without envy or comparison the gifts and strengths of others; to come out of hiding and help others do the same takes courage. So tie up those yellow shoelaces and read on if you dare!

BRAVE:

Balanced, Bright, Bold, and Beautiful

BALANCED

BALANCE IS CRUCIAL TO AUTHENTIC BRAVERY. It is knowing when to take risks and when not to. Balancing listening and speaking, waiting and acting, acting and resting, going first and letting others go ahead, going alone and going with others. It also means knowing when to persevere and when to let go—even though letting go may make us feel that we are letting ourselves or others down. In fact, Concordia University's Carsten Wrosch found that refusing to give up on unattainable goals leads to emotional and physical distress, elevating levels of the proteins that can lead to frustration, illness and exhaustion. She found that girls who learned to cut their losses had higher levels of well-being, making them "more likely to reengage with new, more feasible goals [and] increasing their sense of purpose."[16]

It is also important to find the right balance of compassion for others and compassion for self. We live in an era where many women feel the need to be independent at such a young age and to be good at so many things at once—doing them all effortlessly. The concurrent exponential growth of anxiety, self-comparison, depression, perfectionism, eating disorders, endless ruminating and the accompanying rise of self-medication, sleeplessness, and shallow relationships is truly disturbing.

What is the antidote? The journey is complex and individual-ized, yet some fresh insights and simple steps can truly help. Slowing down enough to practice five powerful rituals can make a huge positive difference. I think of them as A, A, B, B, B.

1. Acts of kindness: Granny was right on this one. Doing something thoughtful for someone else does make us feel better. Make it a habit to do something nice for someone every day—the quirkier, more thoughtful and more secre-tive the better.

2. Authentic feelings: On the other hand, Granny missed the mark if she told you that anger is bad. Or sadness, or any emotion for that matter. Well-balanced people experience the full range of emotions and can identify them for what they are. It is being able to think, "I am feeling angry" and taking the time to process why we feel that way and what we want to do about it is a sign of maturity—not stuffing it down like we may have been taught to do. Being able to say, "I feel sad about the way this conversation is turning, can we talk about it?" is not a weakness. It is the act of a person courageous enough to be authentic. Perhaps hardest of all, being able to say, "I feel envious of you for _____ which I know is crazy because deep down I am super proud of you. I know that your excelling doesn't mean I am lesser so I hope you can forgive me and I promise I will work through it." When we can do this, it is a powerful indicator that we are not only self-aware and self-regulating but also modelling something healthy to others.

3. Beauty: While it is important for BRAVE leaders to be aware of the challenges our world faces, it is equally vital for us to see its beauty. A walk in the woods with a friend, fly fishing in a shallow stream, reading a great poem, trying a new sport or recipe, taking in a concert or a sunset, creat-ing something from nothing, driving a beautiful stretch of road. There is something restorative about making time for people and things that bring us life.

4. Blessings: Positive Psychologists, exploring countless approaches to wellbeing discovered that one strategy out-shines the others for simplicity and effectiveness. Every night before bed reflect on three things that we are grateful for from that day. This practice not only enhances our sleep (helping us cope with whatever the new day will bring) but also decreases negative thought patterns, builds resiliency and develops our sense of wellbeing.

5. Breathing: Intentional, slow breaths not only calm our bodies; they also help us to quiet our anxious thoughts. Try taking a slow breath in through your nose while focusing on filling your lower and then upper lungs. Hold this breath for a slow count of four then exhale through pursed lips while consciously relaxing each part of your body. Repeat in a gentle, calming way. If you forget and begin to take shallow breaths, simply remind yourself and start again.

Reflect: Which of these rituals do you already practice? Are there any you would like to add to your life? Are there others that help you?

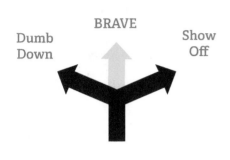

Dumb Down   BRAVE   Show Off

Do you ever question how smart you are? If so, you are less alone than you might think. I loved school and got good grades. However, there were one or two classes in which I did not do well. Never dreaming that it might be at least partially the teacher's approach or the textbook's sterile description of what I now know to be the beauty-filled wonders of advanced math and science, my self-esteem plummeted. I began to self-limit career choices based on fear of failure. Many people do this, but girls, especially in co-ed schools, are more prone to it than their male peers.

By age six, girls in the West have already been socialized to believe that boys and men can be brighter than girls and women.[17] Age 6!

By grade six, many girls have learned to "dumb themselves down" to be better liked by boys and girls alike. Often girls think they must choose between being smart and being liked.

This low confidence shows up most often in the science, technology, engineering and math world. One international study found that "Females tend to report lower mathematics-related self-efficacy than males in almost all countries."[18]

Later, differences in our ways of thinking, processing and decision-making lead to lower scores on male-oriented university tests which reinforces our self-doubt. No wonder many high school and university-aged women struggle with "imposter syndromes"—believing that what we have achieved is some kind of fluke.

Boys who fail at something are more likely to attribute it to lack of effort, while girls are more likely to attribute it to lack of skill.[19] This difference has huge implications in terms of trying again, working harder, goal setting, and establishing the narrative we tell ourselves about our own abilities.

Sadly, low confidence is most common among the brightest and most high-achieving young women.[20] In fact, the more competent you are, the more likely you are to underestimate your abilities.[21] Isn't that crazy! Even adult women often take ten years longer than men to know what they are good at doing.

When asked why there were not more women in top civil service roles, Former Secretary-General of the United Nations, Kofi Annan once said, "I've always been interested in seeing talented colleagues move up, and in my experience, many of them are women. So whenever an opening for a promotion was advertised, I often said to a talented person, 'You should apply for this job.' Women almost universally told me they weren't experienced enough or didn't have sufficient background. I never had a man say anything but 'Thank you, I will apply.'"[22]

While there are links between our competence and confidence, they do not show up in the ways we would think. Ironically, high achievement does not necessarily lead to higher self-esteem for women.[23] In fact, higher achievement may diminish self-esteem as we seek to minimize our success in order to fit in, while at the same time, angst arises about whether or not we have truly earned it.

The ripple effect of this is huge! We know that balanced teams are more likely to see levels of crime, terrorism and corruption decrease and levels of education, health care and overall community health increase.

There is such a high cost to women's low confidence.

As Samantha and I sat in our living room chatting we began to realize that her long-term battle with food was more about fitting-in-ness than fitness. It is easy to think that fitting into our jeans will enable us to finally fit in… or at least serve as a substitute for the accepting relationships we all crave. In a world where beauty seems like an elusive and subjective commodity, we are barely off our training wheels before we realize that Love Handles are anything but, Muffin Tops do not make our morning, and freckles, braces, crooked noses and imperfect skin are the equivalent of a D minus in the tenuous world of popularity.

We live in a world of stereotypes and judgments, an age of appearance anxiety for girls, and this comes with a cost. A global study commissioned by Dove[24] revealed that six out of ten girls opt out of important activities because they are worried about the way they look. Studies in Finland, China, and the U.S. show that a girl's relationship with the way she looks has an impact on her academic performance. Girls who think they are overweight, regardless of their actual weight, have lower grades.

The same Dove study shows how the negative impact of low body confidence continues later in life, with 17% of women claiming they won't go to a job interview and 8% missing work on days when they feel bad about the way they look. We aren't born thinking like this. We learn it in response to the messages at home (the most devastating place), at school, in the media and in the discrimination of hiring, promotions and influence at work.

"Being confident is about knowing what beauty really is."
- Cassie, age 12.

29

Several years ago, our daughter's friend was visiting. After lunch I suggested we all go to the beach. This beautiful young girl refused, saying she did not like anyone to see the little potbelly that showed up after eating. I stared at her in stunned silence. She was about 11 years old at the time. I assured her no one but us would be at the beach. She still refused. Almost in tears, I said, "There are two kinds of women in the world. Some let their fear of other people's opinion determine who they are and what they do. Some would not allow others to have that much power. There are those who go to the beach after eating and those who don't. What kind of a woman do you want to be?" Perhaps cowed by my passion (sorry Love) she slipped upstairs to change. That moment may not have affected her, but it had a huge impact on me. Why had I reacted so emotionally? How often had I let my fear of others' perceptions of me alter who I was, what I wanted, or what I needed to do? Can anyone relate to this?

Reflect: How has your view of beauty and your own body image impacted you?

Our sense of our own beauty determines our belief about how we look—regardless of our jean size, the perspective of others, or the messages others have given. And it would seem that the majority of us view ourselves through a distorted lens. One large study in the US showed no significant relationship between how attractive other people thought a woman was and her perception of her own attractiveness.[25] Girls and women that others see as gorgeous do not necessarily see themselves that way. No wonder so many truly beautiful women feel inadequate. Isn't that also crazy?

The concept of beauty—and who has it—is one of the first messages many women receive. In many parts of the world, baby girls are more likely to be treated as fragile, dressed in pink and described from day one in terms of their "prettiness."

No wonder...

- As young as age 7 children believe they are valued more for their looks than their character.[26]

- 81% of 10-year-old girls are afraid of being fat.[27]

- 91% of women are unhappy with their bodies.[28]

These stats are staggering. And they have serious implications:

- Serious athletes report higher rates of Eating Disorders than their peers.[29]

- 8 out of 10 girls avoid seeing friends and family or trying out for a team. 7 out of 10 will not be assertive in their opinion or stick to their decision when they don't feel good about the way they look.[30]

- Perfectionism, hopelessness and discouragement rates increase through teen years for girls.[31]

Toddler beauty pageants and digitally modified photos are taking their toll. The sexualization of girls in all forms of media is a "broad and increasing problem harmful to girls' self-image and healthy development." It undermines our confidence in and comfort with our own body, leads to anxiety, shame, and difficulty in developing a healthy sexual self-image and has been linked to eating disorders, low self-esteem, and depression—the most common mental health problems in girls and women.[32]

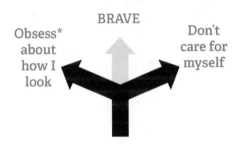

BRAVE

Obsess* about how I look

Don't care for myself

* to preoccupy or worry us almost constantly

It is hard to swim upstream against such powerful waves, but we must ask ourselves if that is who we really want to be.

Reflect: What has informed your view of beauty? How reliable are those sources?

Do you agree that a woman's body image affects her view of her place in the world?

How has your view of yourself influenced your relationships? How has your view of yourself influenced the opportunities you have taken?

Perhaps beauty really is in the eye of the beholder, and we are our own beholder! It is not only the evil Queen in Snow White who asks, "Mirror, mirror on the wall, who's the fairest of them all?" Our insecurities often make us our own worst critic.

Based on this well-known fairy tale, we sometimes lead girls and women through a simple exercise called "Mirror, Mirror." Handing out pens and paper, we ask participants to list and discuss the attributes that they think make women beautiful. Then we post them on a wall around an ornate mirror. Without exception, the lists are lengthy and include things like compassion, confidence, interest in others, personal style, integrity, passion, and sense of humour. There has never yet been one item related to height, weight, color of hair, skin, body shape or anything else to do with body image. Never once in eight years. Most girls and women scoff at the idea when we ask about these characteristics. "Those are superficial," they say, "insignificant." Insignificant? Wow. The disconnect between what we know and what we feel is astonishing.

Exercise: Make your own list of what makes a woman beautiful. Post it on your mirror alongside pictures of diversely beautiful female faces. Study that each morning before leaving home and each evening before going to bed.

How does this help reframe your thinking?

We have a serious problem on our hands.

We need a minimum of 30% girls and women on decision-making teams to see the kind of community and global transformation our world so desperately needs. Yet girls and women with low self-esteem are much less likely to engage in leadership behaviours. We need to do some work on both ourselves and our culture. It will not be easy, but some things are worth fighting for.

Enemies of our Confidence

ONE DAY I WAS MEETING with a small group of smart, young women. One of them was not only well-educated, beautiful, and articulate, but she was also a gifted athlete competing at national levels. Yet, she baulked at the suggestion that she was a leader. I was stunned. Having watched her lead in countless formal and informal settings, I would have assumed she viewed herself as such.

As we have said, bright women are even more likely to struggle with low self-esteem. A report by the Girl Scouts of America found that 7 out of 10 girls aged 8 to 17 have negative opinions about themselves regarding their looks, school performance or relationships—the majority reporting that they felt insecure or unsure of themselves as a result.[33] "Those with GPA's higher than 4.0 were the least likely to say what they thought or disagree with others because wanted to be liked… Girl competence does not equal girl confidence. Nor does it equal happiness, resilience or self-worth."[34] Receiving her high school diploma and being accepted by a university will not necessarily translate into a confidence booster either. In fact, entering college, "she will more likely mark herself lower than men on nearly every measure of intellectual ability (despite no measurable differences in actual ability)."[35]

In that nanosecond, the light bulb went on for me. If this talented, bright, well-loved young woman was struggling with confidence, what must be going on for other women?

3

Surely the maturity gained by experience and successes will build that confidence up during her university years, we speculate. However, research suggests that when she graduates, she will not only be less confident than her male peers but also less confident than when she started her degree.[36] Even in the workplace, low confidence is "a general trait … even of very senior women. They are not yet convinced that they deserve all the opportunities open to them."[37] What?! That is crazy-making! What's more, it affects our ability to influence our world.

> Even at a young age, we know confidence is important, and the lack of it holds us back.

University of California social psychologist Brenda Major has been studying self-perception for decades. She found that men consistently overestimate their abilities and performance and women routinely underestimate them, even though their actual ability did not differ in quality. Still, today, if she wants to suggest a study whose results are utterly predictable, this is the one to which she points.[38] Columbia Business School has found that men on average rate their performance to be 30% better than it is. It is not that guys are cocky and women modest.[39] We each honestly believe the rating we are giving. Many guys seem to have a natural tilt towards over-confidence, or when they doubt, they are less likely to let those doubts paralyze them.

There is something important to be learned here because there is a close link between a woman's perceived self-efficacy and achieving the goals that are important to her. For example, Jessica Grounds, co-founder of Running Start, says that ambitious young women considering a run for office often come to her organization for help. They are not lacking the skill to run but the self-belief that they can.[40] We know that people with higher levels of confidence are more apt to get involved in all spheres of life and leadership and to persevere through the inevitable obstacles that we encounter in life and leadership.

All of this is sending a strong message:

We know confidence is important—and we think we don't have it!

Some of this is a result of the inner critic who lives in our head, telling us that we are too much or not enough. Too tall or too short. Too athletic or too brainy. Too loud or too quiet. Too girly or too masculine. Too sensitive or too strong. Surely not every one of us is too much or not enough!

Where does this low confidence come from?

It starts early. According to clinical psychologist Robin F. Goodman, "Girls' self-esteem peaks when they are nine years old, then takes a nose dive." She says that self-esteem drops in the pre-teen years because there is "a shift in focus—the body becomes an all-consuming passion and barometer of worth."[41] Did you catch that? *Nine years old.* When I first read this startling number, I couldn't help but think of all the precocious 3-9 year-old girls I knew. Then I thought of all the talented young women I knew who are struggling with low confidence. Doesn't it make you wonder what happens in between? And if anything can be done to reverse this disturbing trend?

Listen to the encouragement of the young women coming behind you:

"I don't want to let fear control my life."
- Eva (age 12)

"Don't be the girl whose confidence peaks at age 9."
- Crystal (age 13)

"Step outside your comfort zone."
- Hannah (age 14)

"Risk-taking builds courage."
- Kate (age 11)

"We all struggle. You are not alone."
- Kaitlin (age 13)

Reflect: Have you ever noticed your level of confidence decrease? When was this?

This is real. "By age six, anxiety will be twice as prevalent among girls as boys. As she enters adolescence, she will be twice as likely as her brother to suffer from depression. She will perceive stress more and get less sleep. Her self-esteem will drop across a range of domains: in sports, appearance, and self-satisfaction— to name a few—by late adolescence, her self-compassion will decline to its lowest level of any group of youth."[42] Not only will she experience deeper drops in self-esteem, but she will also take longer to rebound than her male counterparts. A study of thirteen hundred girls in the USA, found that their level of confidence dropped by thirty percent from ages 8-14.[43] Sadly, many studies show that confidence levels bottom out at Grade 9 and stay there.

Reflect: What cultural factors make it difficult for girls and women to be brave?

* Women who have experienced sexual trauma, especially as children, often experience significant self-esteem issues, struggling with shame and broken trust in themselves and others. This may prevail for years if not addressed wisely and compassionately. Finding a good counsellor can really help with this journey.

The good news is that confidence can be built up again.[44] We can choose not to let fear define us. It takes some intentionality and risk to tie up our yellow shoelaces or pop on yellow heels to follow our BRAVE. The positive outcome far outweighs the cost. Yet, even here, we must proceed with caution. To suggest that we must work to become more confident puts the onus back on us, creating one more thing we have to excel at, when in reality it is the culture of families, schools, workplaces and the public forum that must ultimately change.

You may have heard the name, Melba Pattilo Beals. She was one of the nine African-American students who braved the strategic and often cruel opposition of peers, parents, and police to attend an all-white high-school to break segregation in Little Rock, Arkansas in the mid-1900's. Her book is powerfully titled, *I Will Not Fear*, and in it she writes of the influence her grandmother had on her ability to carry on when so many others would have quit.[45]

Reflect: When have the words of someone who believed in you helped you overcome fear?

At particularly difficult times throughout her amazing life this university professor, journalist, NBC television news reporter, author and speaker said, "Over and over again, my grandmother's words came to me: Why go where you're not welcome? Because if you go only where others welcome you, you are confined to surrender to the choices of others. Claim what you want to belong to first."

Looking around at our world and looking deep within ourselves, we have to ask:

How do we find our BRAVE? Where do we find the courage to do the right thing?

It turns out that the answer to this question is both personal and complex. Rooted in our heritage and upbringing, influenced by our personality and experiences, and distorted by conflicting messages from significant adults, media, and friends, our courage is found along a journey that only we can take. It is part of the quest of self-discovery and boundary-breaking every BRAVE woman fiercely (and sometimes fearfully) makes.

Like any epic quest, we make the journey in the company of friends: the heroines of our past and present; the gatekeepers, door openers and eye openers we encounter along the way; and the companions we choose to accompany us.

Our boldness is found in the alchemy of challenges overcome and lessons learned, external affirmation and healthy internal pride, and, critically, in a belief that our life has meaning and that we can make a positive difference in our world. Indeed,

Bravery grows from a belief that something better is possible.

Unfortunately, our bravery has many enemies.

Enemy of our BRAVE #1: Media

When I was 16 years old, I went to summer camp for the first time. As part of the illustrious dish pit crew, we slept in dorm-style rooms above the main dining hall. For some reason, perhaps because I anticipated being homesick, I had brought a scrapbook filled with pictures of friends and family, as well as little reminders of concerts, movies, and other outings. As the summer progressed, little things started to go missing from my, and other people's rooms—bits of money, jewellery, books and my scrapbook. The leaders of the camp found all the items together, hidden at the bottom of someone's trunk. The captions under my pictures had been changed. Someone was retelling my story as her own.

At first, I was hurt and angry, but over time, I began to reflect on what must have been going on in her life for her to feel the need to do this. My heart broke for her. As I look back now, I can also see the irony. High school was certainly not one of my better eras! I struggled to find myself and my people. My body was changing and with it, my confidence. The way I experienced certain classes caused me to question if I had any intelligence at all. I began to doubt my academic ability and future career options. Meanwhile, at home, we were experiencing our own dysfunction. Yet in the scrapbook, filled with pictures from parties, school and family, everything looked good. It was that version of me she wanted—not the real one. Frankly, it was the version I wanted too.

In those days it took weeks to finish a roll of film, get it printed, throw out the inevitable poor quality ones, and paste the good ones into a scrapbook. Only on rare, rainy Saturday mornings when there was nothing else to do, did we get to see someone else's life laid out page after page and compare it to our own.

In today's era of real-time, online scrapbooking, the desire to have someone else's life—or to make our lives look filled with beautiful people, fun activities, mementoes of success, and acceptance—can be dauntingly powerful.

So much has been said about social media that most of us are aware of its pros and cons regarding the depth of relationships and the impact on our sense of self. However, this influence is so subtle and pervasive that a brief reminder of the destructive force of comparison may be helpful. Theodore Roosevelt once said: "Comparison is the thief of joy." How true this is. The problem with the comparison is that there is no way to win. Like riding a teeter-totter with a painful landing on either end, we fall into a sense of superiority and pride (no one likes that person) or inferiority and insecurity (no one wants to be that person). Either way, we are motivated by a desire to prove to ourselves, and others, that we measure up.

Reflect: Why do you think it is hard not to compare ourselves to others?

Reflect: How does social media affect your view of yourself?

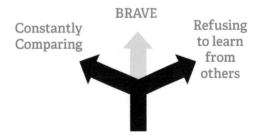

BRAVE

Constantly Comparing

Refusing to learn from others

Reflect: What might a BRAVE response look like?

Reflect: What are the pieces of your story that you love most?

Enemy of our BRAVE #2: Mixed Messages

From birth, in many parts of the world, females are treated as more fragile than their male peers, causing us to self-limit our risk-taking. This treatment robs us of the opportunity of learning from failure and the self-efficacy that pushing ourselves beyond our comfort-zone develops. Many of us have internalized these subtle messages creating non-BRAVE self-narratives that seem impossible to overcome. This self-told storyline and the accompanying voice of our inner critic can be debilitating. Add to this a tendency for people-pleasing, and the pursuit of perfection and it is no wonder we may feel besieged from all sides. Then there is the frustratingly easy tendency to:

- Regret – going over and over what we said or did in the past in endless cycles of second-guessing and re-play. This can quickly develop into guilt about what we perceive ourselves to have done or, even more destructively, shame about who we perceive ourselves to be.

- Worry – negatively anticipating what might happen until anxiety and fear of failure (or success) make it hard to move forward, or even get out of bed some days.

There is a nanosecond of time but a world of difference between healthy self-reflection and debilitating stewing.

Reflect: Do you struggle with either regret or worry? What strategies might help you here?

On top of this, many of us also grew up on stories featuring the following childhood female characters:[46]

- The Pretty Princess – the performer who believes looks and coy behaviours are her best tools to get ahead.

- The Wicked Witch – the plotter, manipulator, and "don't let anyone else get ahead of you" person who moves ahead by ensuring her peers stay down.

- Chicken Little – "the sky is falling" worrier who is so focused on what could go wrong that she cannot enjoy all that is going right.

- The Little Girl with a Curl – the "good girls are quiet and fit in" pleaser who has lost herself in trying to be what everyone else wants her to be.

- Little Red Hen – the "I'll do it myself" passive-aggressive martyr who has given up on asking for help or recognition and hides behind an unhealthy version of independence.

- Rapunzel – the victim who can't rescue herself and—dependent on other, stronger, smarter, or braver types—is caught in an unhealthy version of dependence.

As I read this list, I can't help remembering how often I heard these stories growing up, and how often I told them to my children and grandchildren. No wonder our girls are confused. No wonder we are.

Even the strategies our mothers used to encourage our dreams and empower our behaviour may have worked against us. We are expected to excel across traditionally male and traditionally female roles as well as in all academic, athletic, artistic, and altruistic realms. My experience working with young women, especially privileged young women, agrees with Courtney Martin's assessment that, "girls grew up hearing they can be anything, but heard they have to be everything."[47]

Reflect: Were any of these messages part of your upbringing? If not, what messages were?

Do you recognize any of them at work in your life now?

What alternative archetype might be more helpful to you at this point in your journey?

In an interesting study, 3,000 female college students and professionals were asked about messages they had learned as a child.

86% recalled being told to be nice, to be respectful to others and to be a good student.

68% remember being coached to believe in themselves.

56% to take a stand for what they believed in.

44% to be a good leader.

39% to master a skill.[48]

One woman said, "I wish I had learned that it is okay to be nice and be a leader."

Reflect: What messages did you receive as a child about bravery?

Mixed messages continue into adulthood. Studies in Europe and North America confirm that women in the workplace who are perceived as confident are actually *less* likely to be described as likeable and hirable. These diverse and pervasive influences add up to a confusing landscape for many women. They impact us to varying degrees depending on where we live, our culture, our family context, and our socio-economic position. Globally, they accumulate until many women feel that to be female is to be lesser, *other*, and that to be ourselves is not good enough.

In this context, it takes both reality checks and radical self-compassion to combat the five forces that act like Cinderella's evil stepsisters—seeking to undo us. It may help to understand their motives better.

1. Perfectionism is the shadow side of healthy ambition. It is about trying to stay in control. Yet, when we think about the people we most admire, they often value excellence over perfection. Preparation is good. Excellence is important. However, transformation far exceeds perfection as a healthy and worthwhile pursuit. Ironically, it is easy to confuse the need to be perfect with the desire to please others. One study of over a thousand US college students found that those who strove for effortless perfection actually felt more isolated from their peers due to an extreme need for "self-concealment."[49]

As Brené Brown says, "Rather than question the faulty logic of perfectionism, we become more entrenched in our quest to look and do everything right."

2. People-pleasing is the shadow side of our desire to care for others and belong. The pressure to "be nice" is killing us! Ohio State psychologist Jennifer Crocker says that people who base their self worth on what others think report more stress, higher levels of drug abuse and eating disorders, and lower academic scores.[50] Those who base their self-worth on internal sources such as a strong moral code are much less vulnerable.

Honouring choices that lead to self-respect rather than the constant need to be liked by others, goes a long way to helping us balance these competing voices.

This may require some shifts in our self-narrative until we truly understand that doing the right thing is ultimately so much more loving than doing what someone else wants.

3. Ruminating over the people we did not please, our less than perfect performance, or a breach of our own moral code demonstrates how important these things are to us. As such, it is a window into what we value, but it is the antithesis of healthy learning from feedback or failure. While we know that beating ourselves up is pointless, many of us struggle to break the cycle. Reframing our thoughts by exploring alternative reasons for what happened or insights we can gather from the experience can help us break what can become a compulsive and self-destructive habit. This kind of reframing has proven to be helpful when practiced consistently.

4. Worry seeks to protect us. Bless her heart. But her voice can be so loud she holds us back. Have compassion on her but don't let her be the boss of you. Take her hand, remind her of all the reasons it is important to try and then go anyway.

5. Fear of failure (or success). When considering stepping outside our comfort zone, it is wise to count the cost but equally unwise to get stuck there. One powerful strategy is to step out for someone else. OSU psychologist Jenny Croker has found that when young female college graduates stop thinking about proving themselves or doing well and focus on their team, their peers, a cause, or the benefit of those listening, they had a surprising burst of confidence.[51]

This is where our flip-flops come in. They help us with the reality check and self-compassion piece and remind us that half the equation of movement is flopping. Don't flip out over it. To be human is to be gloriously imperfect. Messing up and 'fessing up is a far better strategy than silence, secrecy, or inaction.

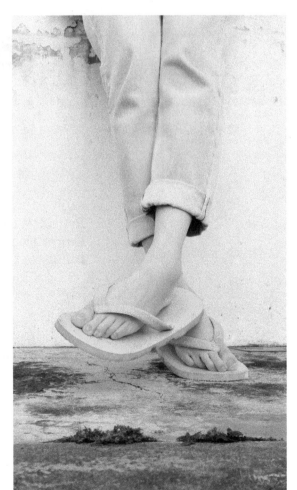

Ironically, in our dualistic society, it can be easy to assume that we can only avoid failure (Evil Stepsister #5) through perfectionism (Evil Stepsister #1). There is an alternative but it is a less travelled way so you may have to carve your own path.

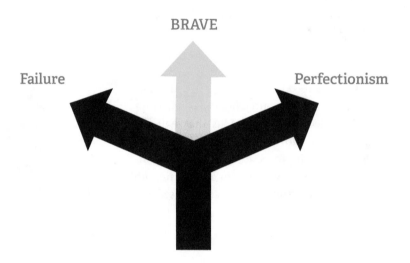

BRAVE

Failure

Perfectionism

Reflect: Which path do you tend towards? How can you learn to lean into both the pain and the beauty of the BRAVE path?

Enemy of our Brave #3 Mean Girls
(...and people generally)

Before talking about meanness, it is important to stress that this is not the same thing as genuine frustration or anger. Many women and girls have been socialized to suppress their anger—a reality many health professionals are linking to our high rates of depression and anxiety. York University professor and special advisor to the Canadian Coalition for the Rights of Children, Cheryl van Daalen-Smith's deep conversations with teens and young women unearthed how often they felt like they had to suppress their anger for the sake of harmony. For many of the girls, the main pressure was to meet preconceived standards.

Girls from visible minority groups experienced additional cultural limits. Those with hurtful sexual pasts—and the sense of deep betrayal that often accompanies this—carry a deep sadness and anger that is unpredictable, and therefore difficult to address. Many girls and young women with visible disabilities encountered additional pressures related to others' perception of them as "full people."[52] Wow. Many of us are wrestling with very real issues. We need people to listen. We need to find ways to express our very understandable anger before it eats us up or comes out as bitterness, resentment or skepticism.

What I am talking about here is not that kind of authentic anger. What I am talking about is meanness.

Have you ever noticed how the people who consistently demonstrate meanness are the ones you would think have the least need to act that way? They are often the people who have everything already—popularity, power, and prestige. Why would they need to put others down? You guessed it. To keep their place in the pecking order and to protect the ideal of what being on top looks like. And, sometimes, to compensate for the emptiness they feel on the inside. It's difficult to have compassion when their actions are so hurtful. It helps to remember that even mean people are on their own journey towards wholeness and that we don't have to be a stepping-stone they stomp on along the way. Have compassion for them if you can but do not listen to them. Don't give them that much power. And don't practice what they do.

While on the topic of meanness, it may be helpful to reflect on the model below and consider how the continual pressure to be nice, perfect and selfless creates unsustainable expectations. Every once in awhile the pendulum may flip, and we find ourselves saying or doing the very thing we abhor. Feeling guilty usually adds sufficient weight to flip the pendulum back. Then the pressure builds again, and the cycle repeats itself. Bah. Is that really who we want to be?

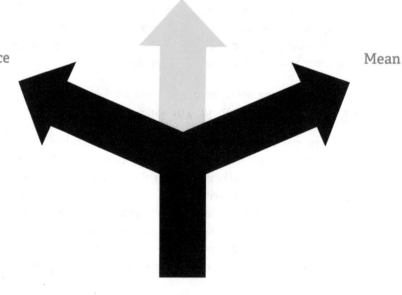

BRAVE

Nice

Mean

Are nice or mean really the only choices? Or is there a BRAVE way that allows us to speak our needs, feel our feelings, maintain our integrity, make our mistakes and let others do the same? To be fully ourselves and encourage others to be as well. To find this path, we can ask ourselves questions like: How can I be both honest and kind here? What will generate a genuine win-win? Why do I feel the need to placate or aggravate in this moment? What is going on in me that is causing things to come out of my mouth that are not the true me?

Reflect: When are you most likely to swing to "mean"? What triggers prompt you to do so? When are you most likely to feel the need to be "nice"? What is the fear behind this?

Another version of meanness is sometimes called the Tall Poppy Syndrome. The metaphor suggests a field of flowers with long straight stalks supporting a single large flower each. When a storm comes, any flowers that are taller than the others are broken off by the wind. Now imagine that field filled with people, each of them unique. When everyone is feeling good about themselves, it is ok for one flower after another to stand out above the crowd. However, when the storms of self-doubt rage, we reach up and break that flower off to make ourselves look better. Crazy? Yes. Common? Unfortunately so.

Is that really who we want to be?

Our favourite flower snippers? Gossip. It makes us feel close to those we are talking with, but there are better ways of doing that without alienating others. Enough said. Is that really who we want to be?

Taken to an extreme, this becomes bullying. Bullying shows up in all kinds of insidious ways. Enough said. Is that really who we want to be?

A more subtle, but equally painful and pervasive version of this? Cliques. No one wants to be on the outside. Enough said. Is that really who we want to be?

Or do we want to be BRAVE? None of these people above are leaders—although they may think they are. They may even have people following them. Yet there is a big difference between a true leader and that. Don't be that kind of person. Address your authentic anger. Discover your uniqueness. Pull out your resilience. Find some true friends. Develop your own voice and speak up about what matters to you. Be BRAVE.

We all need the best version of you.

Sadly, the Tall Poppy phenomenon does not disappear after high school. Why is this? When we lack confidence in ourselves, we seek to pull down those around us. In so doing, of course, we only increase the level of mediocrity and rob ourselves, and those around us, of the opportunity to see greatness. BRAVE leaders resist this childish desire. We start building scaffolds of support when our peers begin to rise.

The antithesis of meanness is radical friendship. True friends not only offset negative messages and experiences we may encounter, but they also act as a catalyst to our growth and a companion on our journey. The word friend in Old English was related to two words: *freond* meaning "to love" and its root word *freo* meaning "free." In Arabic, the word friend was related to two concepts: "the one who accompanies" and "the one who tells the truth." Combining these words and worldviews, we can create a new definition:

> A friend is someone who loves you enough to walk beside you and tell you the kind of truth that sets you free.

Radical friendship reaches across boundaries to build a life-giving community.

Reflect: Who are the friends that help you to see yourself as you truly are and challenge you to be your best self? Where are you creating radical friendships?

59

BRAVE leaders build the kind of radical friendships that can lead to transformation. In fact, meaningful friendships are one of the best predictors and protectors of our BRAVE.

Neglecting the concept of radical friendship comes at great cost. Think of the sense of alienation, the angst of trying to fit in, and the disconnection from our heritage, extended families and neighbours many of us feel! BRAVE Leaders use the skill of radical friendship building to create places of belonging for themselves and others. They understand that without these places, we cannot be healthy or whole. They are also intentional about building in resources to bolster confidence. We will explore these in the next chapter.

Tools to Build Our Confidence

Psychologist Albert Bandura has suggested that four sources feed our belief in our ability to do something. He describes these as:

1. Mastery experiences—which involve personal success and require opportunities to try out new skills and opportunities.

Reflect: What opportunities have you recently taken that built your sense of agency?

4

2. Vicarious experiences—which involve seeing people who are similar to us succeed at things we would like to do. The impact depends on the similarity of the other person—gender and ethnicity are significant factors.

Reflect: Who has inspired you to try something you might not otherwise have tried if you had not seen them doing it?

3. Social persuasion—involves encouragement from others, whose opinion we respect, that says we are capable. Unfortunately, "it is more difficult to instill high levels of personal efficacy by social persuasion than to undermine it."[53]

Reflect: How many confidence encouragers do you have in your life and how much are you listening to them (instead of the voices undermining your personal efficacy)?

4. Emotional status—which involves our ability to stay positive and to manage stress in healthy ways, such that we are more likely to have the personal margin to try new things, take risks and recover or learn from failure.

Reflect: How does your state of mind impact your willingness to move forward on things that are important to you? What strategies do you use to keep you in a positive place?

These are very helpful factors to consider, yet even they do not tell the whole story. For women, a lifetime of mixed messages; a growing awareness of the global mistreatment of women, purely because of their gender; one's personality; one's upbringing; the support (or lack of it) we receive when stepping outside our comfort zone and many other factors make this a vastly complex and deeply personal issue.

It turns out that storytelling and dialogue are two powerful tools for building (or rebuilding) our confidence.

Nigerian storyteller Ben Okri writes, "One way or another we are living stories planted in us early or along the way, or we are living the stories we planted—knowingly or unknowingly—in ourselves. We live stories that either give our lives meaning or negate it with meaninglessness. If we change the stories we live by, quite possibly we change our lives."[54]

> If you don't know the trees you may become lost in the forest; But if you don't know the stories, you may become lost in life.
>
> - Siberian Proverb

Sadly we have lost sight of our stories. As a result, we have lost sight of ourselves. Stories not only craft the lens through which we look at the world, but they also root us in the values, cultures, and histories that help us to see ourselves. Stories create spaces in which we can belong and act as stepping stones to where we could be.

Several years ago, I had the amazing opportunity of taking a sabbatical trip to Scotland—the home of my great-grandparents. I could never have imagined how powerfully I would experience this homecoming. Stepping off the plane and throughout the time I spent there, I felt strangely connected to the land. Sometimes we can find great strength in our heritage.

My mother, two grandmothers, and great grandmother were all Scottish. Women in Ancient Celtic society enjoyed rights that those in Greek and Roman societies did not share. A Celtic woman could own property or get a divorce. She could be a priest, a judge, a doctor, or a poet. She could fight in battle and own her own fighting school. She had the right to rule.

Celtic women maintained their name through the matrilineal line, and I have long identified with my female lineage. Even so, nothing prepared me for the moment when, on a simple day out in the Highlands, our Scottish Tour Guide, stopping at Glencoe, cued stirring bagpipe music and began to tell the story of the massacre that happened there.

Why did I respond so strongly? The beauty of the scene was a contributing factor, as was the effectiveness of the storytelling. However, it went beyond this. I had tapped into something deep and powerful—my story. We can go back into various parts of our personal and cultural stories to find strength and courage.

Since women have been written out of many history books or included only as a footnote, it may be difficult to track our female heritage. Some of us cannot trace our family line. However, if we dig, we can often find sources of strength and inspiration.

Reflect: What stories, traditions, or metaphors from your personal, cultural, or religious heritage do you draw courage from?

Appalachian poet George Ella Lyon's poem "Where I am From"[55] begins:

"I am from clothespins,
From Clorox and carbon-tetrachloride,
I am from the dirt under the back porch.
(Black, glistening, it tasted like beets)."

Using this as a writing prompt I began to write and share this now, with no small sense of vulnerability…

I am Ellen Katherine, daughter of Mary, granddaughter of Florence, of the Clan Macdonald, whose hope is constant.

My ancestors are from the wild Highlands and the rebellious followers of William.

I am also from TV dinners;
the barren, transient lifestyle of suburbia;
and the daily disciplines of silence common to daughters
of shift workers
(noxious Ford plant in our backyard).

Transplanted to the pastures and beaver dams of the
Ottawa Valley:
Children playing as women quilted tents above their heads;
Dappled light through tree lined trails to Chateau Cottage;
Mosquito Island illuminated by moonlight.

Wrenched from that land to the resilient people of the granite rock,
deep lakes, and mighty oaks of Muskoka
(Deep peace that saved me):
Snowshoeing in thigh deep snow past icy waterfalls;
Double swing flanked by cherry blossoms and pine trees;
The call of pathways to water;
Cranberry bogs amidst colors of fall.

More Celtic than Greek; a grandmother, listening; given in love.

I am from a line of women who fight with fierceness;
Pray with faith, and dance with fervor;
who write and read and dare to wonder.

Who laugh and love and care.

Reflect: Write your own "I am from" poetry or prose if you feel so inspired... if not carry on with confidence, knowing other exercises may appeal to you more.

For some, adoption, immigration, estrangement, or loss may make this process difficult. Keep in mind that while we may not have a known blood connection to a place, a home may also be emotional, spiritual, or inexplicable. We may connect to a people or place we have never been, or even to an imaginary realm. We can also be from a place or people who have taken us in, regardless of birth or citizenship. We are from the place where we feel at home, from a people who give us strength.

Reflect: Who are the heroes who have shaped your worldview? Who invites you to believe and speak and act?

Sadly, BRAVE leaders will get knocked around, misunderstood, disillusioned and discouraged. Setbacks will be common. Progress takes longer than we anticipated. Projects will get cancelled. People will betray us. In order to thrive in spite of this, BRAVE Women must learn to embrace the gift of Resiliency. As this gift often comes in unexpected ways and unlikely wrappings, we are wise to watch for its various forms.

BRAVE:

Resilience

WE SEEM TO HAVE DIFFERING AMOUNTS OF RESILIENCE. What throws one person off is taken in stride by another. So, why does one setback cause some people to quit while others rise again and again from hardship or failure?

We know that resilience is both inherited and learned. Through mindfulness and becoming more aware of our reactions and thought processes, we can actually become more resilient. For some people, faith, friends, ors family assist us in the journey. Stanford professor, Kelly McGonigal, has found that connecting with others releases oxytocin during times of stress, making us more resilient.[56] Ultimately though, it is our willingness and ability to access these resources that determines how much we develop this inner strength.

"The biggest predictor of success is not IQ, it's resilience."
- Ellen Johnson-Sirleaf (First woman ever elected President of an African country).

5

"Life is not easy for any of us. But what of that? We must have perseverance and above all confidence in ourselves. We must believe that we are gifted for something and that this thing must be attained."

- Marie Curie, first female professor at the University of Paris and the winner of two Nobel Prizes

Resilience includes the willingness to take risks, to fail, to learn, to get up again, to take a new risk based on what you have learned, to fail again, to get up again.

Merriam Webster defines resilient as

> : able to become strong, healthy, or successful again after something bad happens

> : able to return to an original shape after being pulled, stretched, pressed, bent, etc.

Reflect: Which parts of this definition resonate with your experience?

Resilience is closely linked to hope. Without hope, fear and dis-illusionment creep in, crowding out courage, inspiration, and compassion.

Maria Corazon Aquino, the 11th President of the Philippines, once said: "Faith is not simply a patience that passively suffers until the storm is past. Rather, it is a spirit that bears things—with resignation, yes, but above all, with blazing, serene hope."

Reflect on this quote: How do you inspire hope in yourself and others?

The people we most admire took time to become who they are. These people often experience debilitating setbacks—and kept going. Early in her career, a producer told Oprah Winfrey that she was "unfit for television news." Walt Disney was once fired for not being creative enough. Arianna Huffington, founder of the wildly popular Huffington Post, had her first writings rejected thirty six times. Vera Wang failed to make her first goal of making it to the Olympics and second goal of becoming the editor-in-chief at Vogue, but she is now a famous clothing designer. Business guru Warren Buffet, Apple Founder Steve Jobs and Shark Tank's Barbara Corcoran all had to overcome a terrifying fear of speaking in public before being able to accomplish the work they have done. BRAVE leaders refuse to let fears and set-backs deter them.

Resilience is the sister of persistence and the breakfast of change makers.

Reflect: What is the biggest and best failure you have ever experienced? What did it teach you? How have you learned to take calculated risks? What supports do you have in place for when something bad happens or you get pulled, stretched, pressed, or bent out of shape?

Some of our falls will be big, painful, and public. Others will be small, private, and painful. Pain is the common denominator of falling. And getting back up is the common denominator of BRAVE leaders.

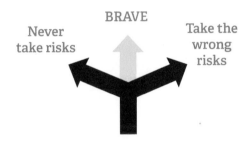

Reflect: What are your strategies for wise risk-taking?

The way we tell the story of what happened is critical. Do we tell it as a learning story fraught with insight and tinged with humour and humility? Or do we tell it (or hide it) as a shame-based story that debilitates? As Sharon Blackie writes, "We make sense of our world and fashion our identities through the sharing and passing on of stories. And so the stories we tell ourselves about the world and our place in it, and the stories that are told to us by others, shape not just our own lives, but the world around us. The cultural narrative *is* the culture."[57]

Reflect: How can changing the way we tell stories change us, and even the world around us?

As Thomas King so wisely notes, a story told one way can heal, and told another way can harm. Stories form both our self-view and our worldview. King asks: "Did you ever wonder how it is we imagine the world in the way we do, how it is we imagine ourselves; if not through our stories."[58]

Reflect: What story from your childhood best demonstrates your beliefs about resilience? Is that story helping you or harming you?

Our resilience is linked to many attributes—our personality, our experience of failure and success, our assumed constraints, and our inner critic. It is also linked to the expectations of our family, friends, school or work setting, and broader culture. In some settings, failure is celebrated. In many others, the fear of failure stops us in our tracks.

One of the biggest hurdles to resilience is our arch-enemy perfectionism. If we persist in thinking we must be flawless, we will be debilitated when we make a mistake or when our imperfections are found out. This undermines our ability to take risks. What a burden to carry.

Some of us struggle more with perfectionism's twin sister—people pleasing. This shadow side of our relational strength can quickly create a destructive firestorm that is difficult to recover from if left unchecked.

The delicate balance of self-care, empathy for others, and stepping outside our comfort zone enables us to release the twin burdens of perfectionism and people-pleasing to become our best selves.

Tools to Develop
Our Resilience

IT CAN BE SO EASY TO NEGLECT OUR SOUL in the busyness of relationships and careers. Not long out of grade school, many women lose touch with what is fun for them and what brings them joy. Our soul and spirit shrivel up as we devote more and more time to caring for others' needs and/or pursuing demanding careers. Taking time for ourselves may seem like an impossible luxury. Yet nothing could be further from the truth. Like the proverbial putting on our own oxygen mask before helping others, caring for our own souls enables us to give out of a much deeper and healthier well.

Where does our BRAVE come from? Surprisingly it grows best in an environment that brings together just the right mix of self-care, empathy for others, and stepping outside our comfort zone.

How healthy is your soul? The New York Times published an article on high-achieving, ambitious girls and their "jam packed schedules," amped up multi-tasking and "profound anxiety." One mother expressed concern that the obsession with achievement could lead to "anorexia of the soul."[59]

Self-care

Empathy for **O**thers

Stepping outside our comfort zone

Reflect: When was the last time you did something life-giving for your soul? If you were to ask your soul what she needs, what would she say? What are the places, people and activities that most nurture you?

Do you ever feel this depleted?

Be careful that you do not neglect your soul in your search for self and service.

How healthy are you physically, emotionally and socially? Are there any changes you could make that would refresh and strengthen you?

Empathy For Others

To have empathy is more than just feeling bad for someone. Empathy is the ability to see things a bit more from their perspective. This is much more difficult to do than we might think. No wonder we so often feel misunderstood. No wonder we so often misunderstand the true external or internal realities of someone else.

One tool that may help enable us to build a 360-degree view of others is the Empathy Map. While no resource can enable us to understand someone else completely, it can help us to slow down enough to notice at least a few more nuances. The tool enables us to reflect on what another person or people group may be thinking, feeling, wanting etc. and can be used in part or whole as a powerful awareness exercise.

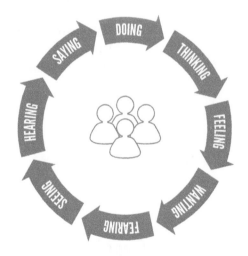

Research has recently revealed that working hard on those areas where we are weaker helps build our resilience as we step outside our comfort zone and prove to ourselves what we can do. In fact, building our confidence requires a mix of staying within our strengths and pushing ourselves beyond them to prove to ourselves that we are stronger than we think. Indeed, even the opportunity to fail, and to fail spectacularly, is a great gift in the development of our BRAVE. It not only helps us to have empathy for others and compassion for ourselves but also proves to us that the world does not end. We can get up and carry on —often stronger.

However, as we have also noted, many women have been raised being told they can do anything but hearing they need to do everything. How then do we find our way through this confusing terrain? One resource that may be helpful is the Cone of Possibility. It was first developed by Lithuanian mathematician Hermann Minkowski to demonstrate that at any given moment in time and space an electron has many (but not limitless) options available to it. The electron can move anywhere within the cone, but to move outside it is virtually infeasible. The further from its current course in the centre of the cone the electron move the more energy will be required.

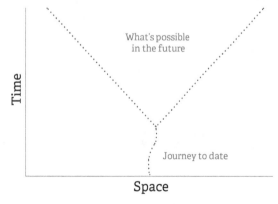

ADAPTED FROM JAMES H. GILMORE AND B. JOSEPH PINE, *AUTHENTICITY*, (HARVARD BUSINESS, 2007).

Applying this concept to our own lives, we can see that at any point in our lives, and with the strengths and opportunities available to us, there are some paths outside the bounds of what is realistic. On the other hand, we can also see that there are many, many options available to us. Pursuing these will require additional energy, commitment and perhaps training, travel or risk-taking for us. The further they are from our current path, the more they will also require us to step outside our comfort zone. The beauty of this model is that it reminds us that we are on a journey and that even a small step to the left or right now can put us on a very different trajectory.

Reflect: Using the Cone of Possibility, track where you are currently heading and the opportunities that small steps in any direction might enable you to move towards.

Take your time with this and return to it as often as you find helpful. Looking at your life through this lens may reveal options you had not considered.

Once these options are listed, move to the tip of the cone and begin to add trajectories of thought and action. What small steps outside your comfort zone could open way more opportunities for you in the future?

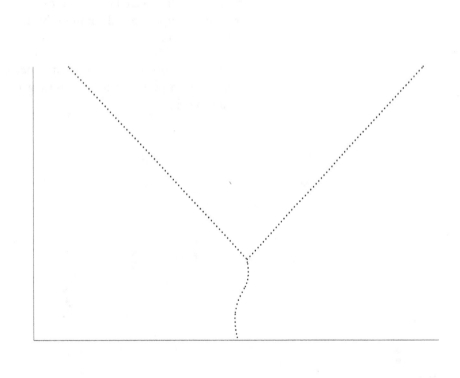

A survey of 1.3 million people about quality of life, found that women are less happy, more rushed, and more stressed than our mothers were and more stressed than our male peers.[60] These findings are disturbing but perhaps not surprising. My experience is that many young women feel like they are drowning.

> Drowning in the expectations they set for themselves.
> Drowning in the expectations that they perceive others have set for them.
> Drowning in details, decisions and deadlines.
> Drowning in complicated relationships.
> Drowning in corporate and community cultures not designed by or for them.

A follow-up study also found that women become even less satisfied with every aspect of their lives as we get older.[61] Is that who we want to be?

Reflect: Are there any areas of your life where you feel like you are drowning? What has been your approach to stay above water? How well is it working for you?

Amazingly, the factor that made the biggest difference in the Buckingham study was the level of commitment women had to be true to themselves—to discover what strengthens them, and to allow this to guide their choices and life journey[62] rather than living a second rate version of someone else's life.[63]

Wow, let that sink in for a moment.

Reflect: Where might I be living a second-rate version of someone else's life? What do I want to do about this?

Where have I given myself the freedom to be completely authentic?

Where do I believe I am making a meaningful difference in the world? What is stopping me from leaning more fully into work that has deep meaning for me?

Fear is a powerful motivator, but as we have noted earlier, love is even stronger than fear. One of the ways we combat fear is by discovering what we love to do.

My Strengths

Many of us have a harder time listing our strengths than our weaknesses. I am not sure why this is. Perhaps it is 1 part true humility (see chapter 1) + 1 part socialized to be modest + 1 part our tendency to minimize the value of things that come easily to us + 1 big part being better at seeing flaws than strengths.

All of us have things that we are no good at and, unless there is genuinely no one else there, would be better left to others. We all have things that we have taken time to develop and excel at. Since we had to learn to do them, these are the things we can and should teach others. We also have a few things, often things we have dismissed as something everyone can do, that represent what we uniquely bring to the table. This could be our ability to make people feel at ease, to see the big picture or to see the opportunity where everyone else sees problems. It could be our creativity, sense of humour, or ability to turn chaos into order. Or perhaps people feel safer when we are around. Maybe we are really good at building things, understanding complex theories, or gauging how people are really doing. The point is, that when it comes naturally to us, we may think it comes naturally to everyone or dismiss it as unimportant. Nothing could be further from the truth.

To find this "something," we can look back into the toy box of our childhood to discover what we have always loved and naturally did. We can also listen to the things people commend us for that we tend to brush off. Sometimes it is helpful to ask a few trusted friends: "If you were starting up a new company and wanted to hire me what unique strength do you feel I would bring to the team?" Listen carefully for insight. Be prepared for answers that you were not expecting.

It is important to spend as much of our time as possible, maximizing this "something" if we want to lean into our ability to most fully contribute. These things may be more difficult to teach because they come so naturally, we don't know how we do them. These are the things we should not often delegate to others. They are our Unique Contribution to the team.

Reflect: What do you tend to dismiss because it comes easily to you or because you assume everyone can do it? What attributes (fun, compassion, friendliness, wisdom, curiosity, openness) come into a room with you? Ask a friend if you don't know.

Reflect: What area of your life could help you to be successful and build your confidence if you could master it?* What do you need to do to prove to yourself that you've got this?

* For many people, public speaking is one of these areas, but you will know best what is holding your confidence back. I went back to school (twice) to prove to myself I could.

It is important to remember that being good at something is not the same thing as getting it perfect. As we keep stressing, perfectionism is the enemy of joy and risk-taking and it is an unhealthy motivator. It kills confidence and divides teams. Yet it is a pervasive problem for many girls and women.

Listen to the following responses of girls to the question, "What is challenging about being a leader?"

Sarah, aged 11, "I feel that because I am a leader, I am supposed to do everything right… that if I do something wrong, I would be a terrible leader."

Madison, age 16, "The hardest thing about being a leader would have to be having everyone looking up to you and trying to be the perfect role-model. You feel the pressure to be perfect, but it is harder than it looks."

"Do not think you can be brave with your life and your work and never disappoint any-one. It does not work that way."

- Oprah Winfrey

Living BRAVEly takes, well, bravery. The bravery to keep trying when it would be so much easier to give up, to experience our own pain and enter into the suffering of the world but not get bitter or sentimental, to live compassionately and authentically, and to choose progress over perfection.

It takes bravery to be fully human.

> To be proud of who we are yet open to growing.

> To be happy when others are pleased and okay when they are disappointed.

> To laugh with joy when we get it right and engage with curiosity when we get it wrong.

> To keep going.

> To risk failure.

Our strength at relationship building can be distorted to interpret failure through the lens of failing our friends, our team, or our family. That is way too much pressure to put on ourselves. Ironically, this pressure often prevents us from trying the very things or speaking up about the very issues that matter most to us and those around us. It is much wiser to recognize that you cared enough to try!

In fact, to be BRAVE will mean some failures. We will need to become okay with this. Reshma Saujani, founder of Girls Who Code, found that teaching girls computer coding helped them become more comfortable with risk-taking and failure. To get a code "right" requires multiple experiments and attempts. Coding teachers noted that at the beginning of the program, boys were much more likely to show what they had accomplished and ask about where they were having trouble. Girls would erase vast amounts of work rather than reveal their flaws. By the end of the program, all of that had changed.

Reflect: Where have you failed recently? How spectacular a fail was it? How did you celebrate it? (Yup, you read that right) What did you learn from it?

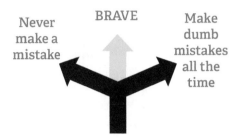

What would you be doing if you were less afraid of failing?

While being resilient does not mean being perfect, it does mean being persistent, and it does mean being trustworthy. Sometimes that means owning up to mistakes. It will be impossible to build transformational spaces without taking some risks and messing up from time to time. Pushing ourselves outside our comfort zone enables us to learn new skills and grow in confidence. It also reminds us that even when we fail, it is not as earth-shattering as we once thought.

95

Owning up to mistakes includes apologizing in a mature way. This apology is very different from the debilitating "I can't believe I did that, how will you ever forgive me? I better say it ten more times and never try that again," whining, and self-recrimination we sometimes impose on ourselves and others. Apologizing maturely means owning what we have done—making it right as much as humanly possible. Learning what we can from it, and then moving on.

Elizabeth Kubler Ros once said, "The most beautiful people we have known are those who have known defeat, known suffering, known struggle, known loss, and have found a way out of the depths. These persons have an appreciation, a sensitivity, and an understanding of life that fills them with compassion, and a deep loving concern. Beautiful people do not just happen."

Truly beautiful people do not just happen. Nor do they shine for themselves alone. Brave, Resilient leaders find the courage to engage in Advocacy and Action for themselves and others.

Reflect: What risk have you been avoiding, and why?

The goal of resilience is not to just survive. The goal is to create cultures of thriving for ourself and others.

Thriving

THREE QUALITIES INTERACT AS OVERLAPPING AND INTERWOVEN pieces to the puzzle of wellbeing. They enable us to be ourselves fully and are more likely to be present when we are believed in by others and can believe in ourselves.

The first quality is a sense of Belonging. People who feel they belong perform better, become more willing to challenge themselves, and are more resilient.[64] While a high value for many people, it may be an even more important factor for girls and women.[65] We develop our values, purpose and self-worth through connection to others.

Many First Peoples, African, South American, Mediterranean, and Arabic cultures share strong values around family, community and hospitality to strangers. Traditional Māori communities were ruled by a group called a *rangatira*. The literal meaning of *rangatira* is "to weave people together"; a definition of leadership that captures the interdependent nature of Māori society.[66] Navaho people of North America have a similar worldview, which they describe as *hozho*.

Many parts of Africa practice *Ubuntu:* a worldview in which leader's "major function" is to "ensure an environment that promotes trust and goodwill amongst their people."[67]

Former Governor-General of Canada, Adrienne Clarkson wrote, "It is society that makes it possible for us to develop ourselves as human beings… we are all born biologically from a union. And it is as part of a group that we learn to belong."

While each of these approaches has different nuanced meanings, they share the common value of connectedness.[68]

There is something powerful in this interdependent view that may resonate with you, as it does with me, although I do not pretend to have mastered its meaning or practice. Dr. Brené Brown asked grade eight students the difference between belonging and fitting in. The answers are so insightful:[69]

- Belonging is being somewhere where you want to be, and they want you. Fitting in is being somewhere where you want to be, but they don't care one way or the other.

- Belonging is being accepted for you. Fitting in is being accepted for being like everyone else.

- If I get to be me, I belong. If I have to be like you, I fit in.

Diversity is an important first step, but radical friendship that creates places of belonging goes way beyond that. "Diversity takes you from zero to one, while inclusion takes you from one to ten."[70]

Research supports the value of inclusion. In one workplace study, "I feel like I belong at my company" was most correlated to engagement in every subgroup.[71] This is especially true for those who are underrepresented numerically.[72]

Reflect: How has your view of independence and interdependence in leadership been influenced by the prevailing worldview of your culture?

Inclusion trumps diversity.

Counter-culturally to the independence-focused society around them in the West, psychologists Jean Baker Miller and Irene Stiver found that we grow through our most important relationships, not through separation. These "growth-fostering relationships allow us to be authentic with our thoughts and feelings in ways that make us feel empowered to deal with conflict or manage change."[73]

"Isolation is a primary cause of human suffering."[74]

Much of our personal and social angst stems from a sense of alienation—a disconnection from our heritage and traditions, as well as our extended families and neighbours. We crave rootedness.

Not having high-quality relationships harms our mental health. "Anxiety increases as social bonds weaken. Societies with low levels of social integration produce adults prone to anxiety." In fact, lack of social trust is the highest predictor of anxiety.[75] And here is the kicker: "The disruption of social ties disproportionately affects women and girls."[76] This makes sense, doesn't it? We know how important relationship-rich cultures are to women and girls. When social ties deteriorate, teams and even societies breakdown.

Like canaries in a coal mine, our angst is more likely an indicator of a society gone crazy than of individuals who cannot cope.

As one author describes it, "[w]hen we feel accepted and validated by others, we reconnect to our inner selves and to the world around us… For women leaders, the affirmation and support of a larger community are still uncommon… Women leaders… are constantly reminded—subtly and not so subtly—that we are not truly welcome as we attempt to impart perspective or advocate a point of view. This type of repeated rejection has a profound effect. We doubt our own ideas, intuition, and knowledge. We lose our self-esteem, confidence and desire to contribute."[77]

Even highly valuing friendship can impact our already faltering self-confidence. Especially when our self-esteem can become linked to how many friends we have or how life-giving our relationships are.

Ironically, even when things are going well for us, we may adopt the common female strategy of talking about personal problems to intentionally diminish our power and equalize any perceived differences with our peers.[78] We do not want to stand out. However, cutting ourselves down leads to unhealthy patterns for others to follow and decreased self-confidence all around. Sadly, "women not only diminish their self-esteem through negative self-talk; they also fail to compensate for it by building themselves up when they experience success. We usually attribute our accomplishments to factors outside ourselves."[79] If you have ever been tempted to act in this way or to think the only options are cockiness or self-diminishment perhaps this helps us to see that there is another way. The BRAVE way we illustrated earlier—the humble way we discussed in the opening pages of this book. This is one of those places where we see how important the path we choose can be.

Reflect: Do you ever use negative self-talk to fit in? How frequently? How might this be influencing your view of self?

What fear or belief system is this masking?

What do you think might happen if you and your friends committed to a different way?

BRAVE Leaders create places of belonging for themselves and others.

Reflect: Where do you feel that you truly belong?

Where are you creating true places of belonging for yourself and others?

While some cultures, families and individuals seem fixated on independence, we actually all exist along a continuum of dependence, independence, and interdependence. To thrive, we must be set free to dance back and forth across this continuum at will.

Dependence_____Independence_____Interdependence

Think about it. We are all born dependent on a caregiver. Over time, most people with sufficient resources and support (and often even without them, which is amazing when you think about it) develop a healthy sense of independence.

Independence is a good thing. Every able person should learn to fix, build, create, make decisions, plan, speak, and travel on our own. We do a great disservice to ourselves—and our children—if we teach them otherwise.

In the West, we value independence as an ultimate goal. Yet deep down, we understand that there is something transformational beyond this stage: the synergy of healthy interdependence. This includes the ability to give and take, to care for and be cared for, to love and be loved, to teach and to learn.

Regardless of what your kindergarten teacher said, dependence is not always a sign of weakness. We are dependent on air, water and, quite frankly, lots of other people and things. Leaders who try to do it all themselves are not only more likely to fail but also have also totally missed the importance of collaborative leadership. Dependence, as long as it is not co-dependence, is not necessarily bad.

Across the past two decades, the Search Institute, and others have demonstrated that the number and intensity of high-quality relationships in a young person's life is linked to a broad range of positive outcomes.[80] Of course, some of us like to have two or three close friends and others love to have dozens.

Reflect: What works best for you?

Healthy interdependence requires a whole set of skills that are not taught in school. When it comes to our emotions, we may think our only options are to minimize them or allow them to escalate. Multiple times a day, we may stand at this crossroads: fearful of being overly emotional or emotionally clueless. Societal pressure, our desire to please, or our hurt and frustration may tip us toward less healthy choices, but in reality, there is the option of a truer, wiser, BRAVER way.

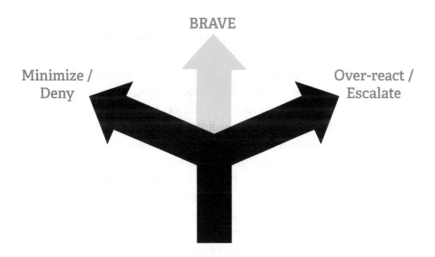

BRAVE

Minimize /
Deny

Over-react /
Escalate

Reflect: What would this BRAVE path look like for you?

* Childhood trauma can lead to attachment injuries resulting in rigid independence or, alternatively, over-dependence on others. Finding our way through this can be challenging but a good counsellor can really help.

While messages, context, and personality can make consistently choosing the BRAVE path hard, recent insights from brain science reveal that there are strategies that can help us. One of the simplest and most profound is to ask ourselves higher-level questions, forcing us to use the parts of our brains that can most help us in that moment. When we focus on the big picture—who we really want to be, the kind of relationships we want to have, the kind of outcomes that are important to us—we can minimize the tendency to spin into minimizing or escalating our emotions.

Reflect: When is it most challenging for you to choose the BRAVE path? What are some examples of higher-level questions that can you could ask yourself when you stand at this crossroads?

Walking the BRAVE path requires self-differentiation, a concept introduced by Murray Bowen decades ago yet still not well known. Self-differentiation includes both our innate ability to separate our thoughts from our emotions; and our external-interpersonal ability to differentiate our experience, thoughts and emotions from others. A self-differentiated person is fully in tune with their own and others feelings but not ruled by them. When we are practicing this concept well, we are able to observe both our emotions and our rational thinking, reflect on what we see and choose how to maximize the validity and strength of both. Differentiated people are deeply in tune with their emotions *and* strongly rational and logical. They also walk the razor's edge of deep caring while not carrying their burdens in ways that are unhealthy or disempowering. The Ancient Mothers and Fathers of the Christian faith tradition referred to this ability as Loving Detachment, enabling one to care without becoming enmeshed. This is a difficult yet beautiful calling.

Undifferentiated/Differentiated Self

Read over the following chart.

Undifferentiated	Differentiated
Easily offended	Self-managing
Slow to recover	Resilient
Reactive	Proactive
Underhanded	Open handed
Stubborn	Generous with perspectives
Demanding	Appropriate and generous allocation
Resistant to reason or love	Open to reason and love
Unbending	Flexible
Black and white thinking	Open to ambiguity
Tendency to blame	Takes responsibility
Critical and fault-finding	Listens and seeks to understand
Uptight	Open and relaxed
Defensive	Open with nothing to hide or defend
Overly Competitive	Appropriately competitive/ collaborative
Contemptuous	Curious
One sided thinking and solutions	Seeks diverse perspectives
Pulls away during conflict	Leans in during conflict
Get angry during conflict	Finds conflict interesting
Seek quick solutions	Open to longer term processes

Source: Ellen Duffield, adapted from Peter Steinke, *Healthy Congregations* (Rowman & Littlefield Publishers, 2006), 20.

Reflect: Which of the undifferentiated mindsets or behaviours are you most likely to default to when not in a good place? What are the motivators behind this? We go to these places because they "give us" something. If we were not getting something out of it, we would not go there. What are you getting out of going to this undifferentiated place? Is this who you want to be?

You may notice that the attributes and behaviours we may display when we are undifferentiated are undergirded by fear—fear of failure, fear of letting others down, and the big ones: fear of exposure or loss of control. Differentiation, on the other hand, is marked by openness, vulnerability, generosity of spirit and an abundance mentality. Whenever we see ourselves acting out of the left-hand column, it can be helpful to ask what is going on at a deeper level to enable us to uncover and address the root.

Reflect: Look at the words in the right hand column. Which ones represent you at your best?

What is the correlation between the two lists you have chosen?

Imagine that the two columns represent two sides of a stream and that you want to find a way across. What stepping-stones would you need to put into place to move towards a healthier differentiation in the area you want to work on? Feel free to choose a different word to represent your goal in the right-hand column if the one listed next to yours does not accurately represent the healthier side of you. List the stepping-stones and develop a plan for putting them in place in your life.

We have probably all set New-Years-Eve-type resolutions to change our behaviour. We begin with great resolve only to find ourselves back where we started within weeks. This is often due to a combination of external challenges—such as other people's expectations or lack of time—and internal challenges—such as our inability to prioritize. Beneath these challenges lay even deeper ones that relate to the benefit we are getting from not changing. These may include things like a sense of unworthiness, the cost of change, the opportunity to reinforce our skeptical view of the world, other competing priorities, or listening to our inner critic. These barriers can be deep and very real. Sometimes we need the help of friends, a coach, or a counsellor to help us unpack them with the right mix of self-compassion and resolve.

Reflect: What are the barriers (internal and external) that might make it challenging for you to access these stepping-stones?

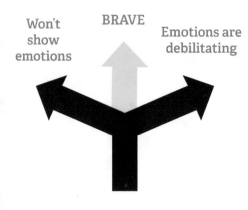

Won't show emotions

BRAVE

Emotions are debilitating

While on the topic of emotions, it may be helpful to remember that women sometimes get accused of being emotional—or "overly emotional"—whatever that means. In my experience, it most often refers to tears. Meanwhile, a whole range of other emotions (laughter, anger, frustration, disappointment) are acceptable. Doesn't that seem odd to you?

Looking at this more objectively—by understanding what tears do—may help us to put aside the frustration and shame some of us experience with tears. Our eyes create three kinds: basal tears that coat our eyes with a thin salty film that provides antibodies and moisture and repels irritants; Reflex tears that flood our eyes to wash away irritants that do get in; and Emotional tears that flow when we feel grief, compassion, joy, laughter or awe. They remove toxins, lower our heart rate and stress levels, and stimulate "feel better" endorphins. Tears really are amazing. Yet in many societies, they are considered a sign of weakness and something that needs to be controlled or managed. Once again, there is a third way. The BRAVE way of self-differentiation that enables us to validate our tears while not being so debilitated by them that we cannot fully contribute to a conversation. A good counsellor or coach can help us work through this in healthy ways.

Reflect: Who could help you reflect more deeply on this and develop strategies to move forward? What's your plan to take advantage of this opportunity?

The second piece of the Thriving Model represents our sense of self. Our identity. Our inner core. Our Being. The search for this True Self is a lifelong, deep, and empowering quest. It involves both outer experiences and inner reflection.

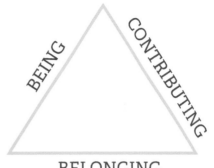

This search is not easy, but it is essential. Women with a strong sense of self are less intimidated by others, less likely to adapt themselves to fit in, less likely to need to stand out or hide away, yet more likely to speak up and stand up according to their values. As we have previously explored, they are also more likely to fess up when they make mistakes while not being devastated to discover they are not perfect. Women with a strong sense of self are more differentiated and emotionally healthy. These skill sets and mindsets build our resilience and deeply influence our ability to create environments where others can thrive.

"Go into yourself and find out how deep is the place from which your life springs."

- Rainer Maria Rilke

Our sense of self grows from so many places—our values and core beliefs, our interests, personality and training, our experiences and preferences. It is influenced by the broader worldview and by the way our primary caregivers thought of themselves and us when we were children. It includes knowing what makes us laugh, what makes us angry, and why. As it matures, our sense of self moves beyond knowing who I am to include knowing who *we* are. This does not mean that a healthy sense of being is built purely on our perception of belonging—otherwise, it crashes when we feel excluded. Belonging is more deeply rooted than acceptance into any group.

In a world where people are besieged with distorted versions of acceptance, BRAVE Leaders make room for people as they really are and space for who they are becoming. This is deep work that begins with us. It should be treated as both sacred and unpredictable.

113

Reflect: What words and word pictures would you use to describe your unique identity? How well do you feel you know your inner self and what matters to you?

The third piece of the model symbolizes our unique contribution. By this, we mean not just our work—both paid and unpaid—but also the signature attributes that we bring with us every time we enter a room. These are the strengths that we may not even be aware of that we naturally bring. Many of these grow out of our Being—our way of thinking and speaking, our core values and experiences. They may also grow out of our Belonging—our upbringing, cultural norms, networks, role models, and mentors.

Exercise: Consider the link between who you are (at your core) and what you do and bring. How does one reflect and enhance the other?

When we think about what we bring to the table, it can be helpful to remember that adding value *through* our contribution is very different from finding our value *in* our contribution. Similarly, we must learn how to differentiate contributions that are motivating and life-giving from versions that can be insidiously dangerous to ourselves or others. Our old enemies of perfectionism, fear of failure, people-pleasing and the felt need to prove ourselves can come flaring up here with a vengeance if we are not careful.

Reflect: Do you feel that you can bring your best contributions to the world through your various paid and unpaid work opportunities and relationships? If not, how might you develop those opportunities for yourself?

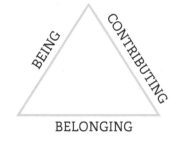

Reflect: Looking back at the Thriving Model, think about how balanced and healthy your life is in each of these areas. Is one area more developed than another? Is there one area where would you like to do some work?

ALIENATION

FALSE SELF

LABOUR

Sadly, it seems we live much of our lives in a distorted version of thriving. Our sense of Belonging may be replaced with a sense of Alienation. Our True Self may be overshadowed by a False Self who shows up to help us to fit in or survive but soon traps us into someone else's version of who we should be. Meaningful Contribution can become distorted into aimlessness, thankless toil, or work-a-holism.

Reflect: Is there any place where you feel alienated? Why?

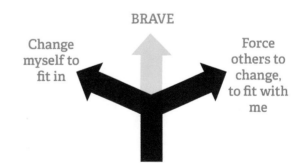

BRAVE

Change myself to fit in

Force others to change, to fit with me

Reflect: Where does your false self tend to pop up? Why?

Where do you struggle with over-commitment or, alternatively, finding work that gives you joy and a sense of purpose?

Our core work is to create places of **Genuine Belonging** where people can find their **True Selves** and bring their **Best Contribution.**

Reflect: How are you creating this kind of culture around you?

BRAVE:

Advocacy and Action

8

THE A OF BRAVE IS like the point of an arrow. When shot by a master archer from a beautifully crafted bow, it pulls the rest along with it. I am certainly no master, but I do love archery. There is something empowering about pulling back that string, taking a deep breath to calm and centre myself, turning the elbow of my bow-holding arm out and releasing the fingertips touching my cheek. The sound of the feathers moving through the air. The thud of the tip as it hits its mark. The competition against myself to improve. The silencing of all the other voices that seek to rattle around in my head. The smell of the trees in the distance and the sun on my face. What's not to like? But do my arms ache after a long session and do I get frustrated with myself as I consistently get worse before I get better. Archery is hard work. And so it is with Advocacy and Action.

The truly transformational dialogues and deeds that can replace silence and suffering don't come easily.

For the ancient Hebrew, words and deeds were so closely linked that word could more accurately be translated *wordeed*. It was unthinkable that someone would say one thing and do another. It was understood that we speak loudly through our deeds. Similarly, advocacy and action are like two sides of one coin. Two interlocking pieces. Two powerful tools in the tool belt of BRAVE Leaders.

Advocacy is a powerful thing. We can envision it in two transformational ways.

1. To advocate with and for others, not just in the speaking-up-for-those-who-cannot-speak-for-themselves kind of way we define advocacy, but as something much deeper, more challenging, more lasting and more transformational.

2. To advocate for ourselves, not in a "these are my rights" kind of way, but rather, coming to the table with a thoughtfully considered opinion in one hand, ready to receive and learn from other perspectives in the other.

Many of us had parents or other caregivers that advocated for us but did not teach us how to advocate for ourselves. If these models embarrassed us—"Mom, please stop saying that!"—we may have developed distorted pictures of what advocacy is all about. Additionally, many of us have been socialized to think that advocating for yourself is selfish. Nothing could be further from the truth. When we don't speak up about what we believe, think and need, we place the unrealistic expectation on others that they will somehow, miraculously, know. Then we become upset when they don't. Such unmet expectations and assumptions can trigger resentment, disillusionment and a host of unhelpful thoughts, emotions and behaviours. This can lead to the pendulum reactions between being "nice, selfless and perfect" and being "mean, selfish and bad (and not in a good way!)" that we discussed earlier. Rarely do we pause to reflect on the irony that we expect others to identify our true needs when we ourselves cannot even name them.

This is especially true with our emotional needs. Like a beach ball pushed deep underwater, these emotions fly up with unexpected force when we, and others, least expect them, leading to further spirals of guilt, shame and repression.

Ironically, while this behaviour may seem selfless, it has been shown to reduce our levels of true empathy for others. Meanwhile, it increases aggressive and passive-aggressive behaviours, reinforces our tendency to self-silence, and diminishes our sense of personal integrity. Is that who we want to be? It may take some intentional retraining to become comfortable with being able to name our emotions, trace their root, express them in non-judgmental "I" statements and be able to separate truly personal attacks from helpful feedback and diverse perspectives.

Socialized to "be nice," many of us fear expressing legitimate anger, sadness, envy or fear, so we mask these emotions behind false statements that proclaim we are happy, fulfilled and fine when in fact we are anything but fine.

123

Understanding what is happening in our brain during times of high emotion helps us to regulate our response. The amygdala (sometimes called our "lizard brain") is a small organ within the brain. Whenever it picks up a signal (real or imagined) that we are being threatened, it pumps Cortisol into the prefrontal cortex, reducing our logical processing faculties by up to 66%. Two things flush this Cortisol out and enable us to calm down: time and oxygen. Asking for a few minutes to regroup, walking away, and taking ten deep breaths helps us to reset.

Train Wreck

We have all experienced it. We are walking down the street, and someone we know passes by on the other side without waving or saying "hi." In these situations, our brain quickly jumps to conclusions—often negative conclusions—about why this happened. Very often some version of blame emerges: "She hates me," or "I did something wrong last Tuesday," when, in fact, there may be any number of reasons why she passed by. Unfortunately, once our brain has conclude, we see everything through that lens. Now we start to feel some emotion (frustration, anger, disappointment, hurt). These emotions and this lens link quickly to other similar experiences we have had in the past, views we have of ourselves, fears, our sense of inadequacy, harsh words others have said and a host of other variables. All of this baggage, like cars on an out-of-control freight train, come crashing in with us when we see that person the next time.

Not knowing why we just reacted the way we did, the other person now begins collecting their own freight train full of information, misinformation, feelings, past experiences, fears, etc. until they build up enough steam to also storm into our next meeting.

If this continues unchecked, we will have a communication train wreck—usually with no just cause. Not all people explode in these kinds of situations. Some people clam up—making it difficult to know what they are thinking or what freight they are bringing.

Consider how much more this happens in more serious misunderstandings, differences of opinion, and observed behaviours. Imagine how widespread trauma and historical abuses of whole people groups can lead to train wrecks of horrific proportions unless wisely directed.

125

When we can channel the energy of the train into a momentum that moves us all further ahead (rather than allowing it to collide), there is incredible possibility. But controlling the train can be profoundly difficult in complicated conversations; especially those with hurtful histories. Consider how much further we could go if we were open to truly unpacking all the good, bad, and ugly baggage we carry with us to allow for deeper understanding. We begin to see how complex many of the interpersonal situations we face are and how deeply we need vulnerable, skilled and wise communicators.

Reflect: How skilled are you at being aware of your own baggage and helping diffuse situations by redirecting the energy you and others bring to conversations?

Our goal in thinking about this is not conflict avoidance. If "conflict is normal in human relationships, and conflict is a motor of change,"[81] perhaps, the constructive change that comes from certain conflict is transformational.

Reflect: How does thinking about conflict resolution as conflict transformation reframe the way you look at it?

Sometimes conflict can get between us:

However, envisioning conflict as something in front of us that we can solve together,

Me ⟵⟶ You

Conflict

can transform the way we look at it.

When it comes to conflict, we sometimes think there are only two options—fighting or acquiescing. This suggests two approaches:

Acting aggressively—in this case at least, proving my point is more important than pleasing people.
Acting passive—pleasing people is more important than proving my point.

There is a third way to think about differences of opinion. The BRAVE way suggests that ensuring all perspectives are fairly considered is more important than either people-pleasing or proving my point. Using this path can lead to insights previously not considered.

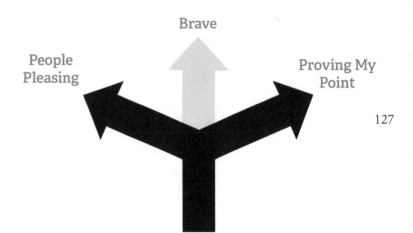

127

Consider the alternative. The pressure to be nice and passivity are often linked. Passive responses may be difficult to read in conversations since we may be truly engaged. Conversely, we may be afraid to give an opinion, passive-aggressive, more likely to talk after the meeting than during the meeting, not willing to contribute because we are angry, or quietly sabotaging the process. Either way, passive participants are essentially saying, "I don't want to contribute an opinion or make a decision" or more simply, "You win."

Aggressive responses express that, "I have an opinion and will out-talk (or out-shout) you if I need to" or, more simply " I win." Aggressiveness may come across as noisy, dominating the conversation—or as manipulation through a power-play un-willingness to share. Have you ever noticed how some people, just being in the room, shut down the conversation? That tells you something!

BRAVE leaders express with their words, body language, and mindset, "I have some thoughts that I think will add to our conversation and I am truly open to hearing other perspectives as I want to learn." This approach respects both our own, and others' voice.

Reflect: Which path do you tend to take in conflict-rich situations? Is that approach serving you well? Is it who you want to be?

Merriam-Webster defines an advocate as a person who argues for or supports a cause or policy; a person who works for a cause or group; a person who argues for the cause of another person in a court of law.

No wonder we often think of an advocate as someone who speaks or acts on behalf of someone who cannot. While this definition may be helpful, and true in some cases, it is equally untrue and unhelpful in many others. Especially when it reflects a paternalistic approach. Any intervention (Latin for "to come between, to interrupt") must be approached with great care lest we come between and interrupt more than intended.

"How can we help make things right?" and "How have I unwittingly been contributing to the problem?" are often a more helpful lens than "Who is right?"

Ellen Johnson-Sirleaf, who we mentioned earlier, understood the importance of helping people become their own advocates. She once famously said, "The people of Liberia know that government cannot save the country—only their own strength, their determination, their creativity, their resilience and faith can do that."

Similarly, Indira Gandhi, the first female prime minister of India, wrote: "A nation's strength ultimately consists in what it can do on its own, and not in what it can borrow from others."

It is generally wiser to think of advocacy as coming alongside others to hear their story and, where appropriate, support their priorities or processes. Otherwise, even with the best of intentions, we may set up patterns of disempowerment and dependency rather than empowerment and interdependence. This is sometimes referred to as "Learned Helplessness" and is the antithesis of the true work of an Advocate. Not to mention that it is disrespectful not to allow people to speak for themselves what they believe, need and have to contribute.

To be an advocate for others is first and foremost to think deeply about what it means to be human.

Reflect: Although this may seem like a purely philosophical exercise, I encourage you to think deeply about this before moving on. What does it mean to be human?

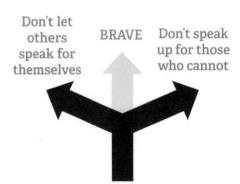

We share so much in common. Yet, at the risk of stating the obvious, we are also more culturally and personally diverse than we might at first imagine. Seeing the world through such different lenses, we, therefore, see different things as important, right, good, fair or just. BRAVE Leaders understand and embrace this by valuing diversity, creating inclusive spaces and intentionally challenging and expanding our own worldview.

> Each mind is a different world.
> Mexican proverb

Tools to Practice Advocacy and Action

9

Mahatma Gandhi once said, "The true measure of any society [or community] can be found in how it treats its most vulnerable members."

Reflect: Do you agree? Disagree?

How do you see this principle working out in your community?

BRAVE Leaders know they cannot do everything. Have you seen the Kia Superbowl ad that features Melissa McCarthy attempting to save a whale, a tree, and a charging rhinoceros? It brilliantly points out how quickly we can burn out if we try to take on every important issue. Choosing what not to do is an important skill and discipline. In a world with so many needs, it can be difficult to know where we best fit in. When it comes to unearthing our place and our passion, I like to suggest that we think like detectives—looking for Motive, Means and Opportunity.

Ask: What is your Motive for addressing this issue? How has it influenced you? For example, many people dedicate their lives to science or medicine after seeing a loved one pass away from an illness that research or treatment might have prevented or cured.

Ask: What Means do you have at your disposal? Time, resources, expertise? How might they best be used?

Ask: What Opportunities are within your reach? A school seeking someone to read to kindergarten students? A nursing home with lonely clients? A fundraiser in your community hall this Friday? A friend already involved in something worthwhile that you could support? A global issue you could investigate further?

There are certain opportunities to improve our world that we will connect to because of our own experience or that of someone we care about. Others jump off the page of a newspaper in unexpected ways or are encountered while travelling. Whatever the opportunity, commit to it enough to see at least a difference in your own behaviour and perspective. It is imperative, however, that this happens without developing a judgmental attitude toward others who are now less enlightened than yourself.

Other opportunities can be shared by us all. All BRAVE Leaders can explore how selfishness, greed and entitlement are—perhaps unknowingly—influencing us: How my purchasing is affecting child labourers halfway around the world, how my over-consumption is contributing to the depletion of resources, how my preference for fresh strawberries out of season is adding to our carbon footprint...my...my...my.

You may have seen the TV ad featuring a little girl surrounded by her toys saying "Everything you see before me is mine." While entertaining, the message is also disturbing. The craving for possessions and the trap of entitlement start early... mine... mine...mine.

The sooner we acknowledge this, the better. However, we cannot let guilt and regret trap us into overreaction or inactivity. If you are one of the fortunate who, like me, rises each morning without fear of starvation or threat of violence, we can learn to practice the following:

The opposite of greed is generosity—even a small act can have a huge impact.

Reflect: Where does greed have a hold on you? Where has practicing generosity brought joy and freedom for you?

The opposite of selfishness is kindness—it never ceases to amaze how simple acts of kindness lead to a breakthrough.

Reflect: What is the difference between being nice and being kind?

The opposite of entitlement is thankfulness—make noticing and appreciating the little things a daily practice.

Reflect: What practices of thankfulness do you practice?

The opposite of injustice is dignity and respect—justice is always personal.

"Justice is to be measured by the extent to which people honor their obligations to live in relationships that uphold the equal dignity and rights of the other."

Reflect: How does this description of justice inform your thinking?

The opposite of conflict is peace, and ironically, peace is worth fighting for—but the weapons of peace are very different from the weapons of war.

Reflect: What weapons of peace do you regularly use (even though you may not have thought of it like that before)? How could you leverage these even more powerfully?

And perhaps most importantly, the opposite of denial is awareness. We do not need to wallow in what is wrong with the world. However, if we are surrounded people who experience the world as we do, we can easily slip into groupthink, self-justification, and compromise. Thinking ethically, and creating environments where all people can thrive takes great intentionality in our fast-food, waste-promoting, issue-of-the-month world. But what a great thing to think about!

Reflect: How do you keep yourself aware of what is going on in the world?

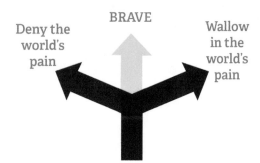

Deny the world's pain — BRAVE — Wallow in the world's pain

Just to clarify. This does not necessarily mean switching vocations. This is about becoming more intentional about using the opportunities that are before us.

We are the culture shapers of our world.

138

Narrowing the options for our places of best contribution we find there is a sweet spot where Passion and Excellence overlap with Need.

If we are not passionate about it we will burn out.

Without key skills, we will be ineffective.

If there is not a genuine need then... well, what's the point?

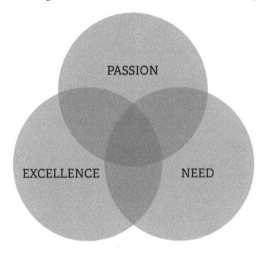

Reflect: Where do passion, excellence and need overlap for you?

Passion is also closely linked to pain. In fact, where pain and passion collide our calling is often found.

Reflect: How has suffering shaped the unique contribution you bring?

Reflect: How has the beauty or the vision of something better shaped the unique contribution that you bring?

Our contributions may look different than we expected. Sometimes they take years to emerge. Other times they appear as a tiny seedling, so fragile we doubt their ability to have influence. Sometimes they show up as suffering cradled in insight. Yet, speaking now as a grandmother, I promise you these unlikely appearances often have the most meaning of all.

However, there are dangers to be avoided. Some of these dangers arise from idealism mixed with the desire for personal satisfaction or immediate gratification. This may take many forms.

- The belief that we can overcome complex issues with a single strategy or a short-term fix.

- Involvement in causes that are trendy or make us look good.

- The desire to build a new organization rather than partner with those already working in the area when there is no real need to do so.

- Insisting we know what needs to be done without taking the time to live in the context and learn from those who do.

- The temptation to give up too soon.

- Settling for a lesser vision in order to see it accomplished more quickly or easily. Or alternatively, striving for perfection, refusing to accept good enough when good enough truly is good enough.

- Insisting something unfold the way we envisioned when we started, forgetting many visions develop as new insights are gleaned along the way.

One antidote to this final danger is to think like a rock climber. A rock climber sees the immensity of the mountain to be scaled. They plot a course, ask those who have gone before, read the weather, and prepare for every contingency. Even with this level of intentionality, the rock climber knows there will be times when they need to go sideways to find a better hold, or backwards to re-assess a different route. Even then the rock climber counts on and commits to, their team to get them through when things get tough. BRAVE leaders approach their life with a similar mix of zeal and flexibility.

We live in a beautiful yet broken world—a world in need of thousands upon thousands of BRAVE influencers. How can it be that so many bright, well-connected and committed people have not been able to wrestle some of the huge challenges and injustices of our world to the ground? How is it that in this generation:

- 80% of the world lives on less than $10 per day; more than 20% on less than $1.25. Hunger is the number one cause of death in the world with 22,000 children dying of poverty every day. 750 million people are without adequate access to clean, safe drinking water.[82]

- Estimated numbers of people caught in Human Trafficking range from 20 to 32 million people—as much as the population of Canada. And in Canada, as in many parts of the world, 25% of those trafficked are minors. Even more startling is the fact that 50% of victims are aged 18-24 and so are 41% of perpetrators.[83]

- At our current rate of consumption and waste, primarily in the West, we need 1.69 planets to sustain our existing population.[84] More than 800 animals (that we know of) are extinct and another 19,000 are endangered or vulnerable.[85]

- Worldwide, 35% of women will endure some form of violence.[86]

- While the number of armed conflicts appears to be deceasing, the number of deaths from each conflict is escalating. Meanwhile, the world spends just $1 on conflict prevention for every $1,885 it spends on military budgets.[87]

Not to mention worldwide issues of neglect, loneliness, mental and physical illness, overcrowded prisons, racism, loss and grief, elder abuse, the breakdown of families and communities, political unrest, addictions, and bullying.

We are going to need more creativity, more diversity of thinking, more inclusivity and collaboration. We are going to need more and more of us to speak up. BRAVE Activists and Advocates, therefore, understand the importance of developing a powerful Voice that is rooted in our Values.

BRAVE:

Voice

The human voice is the organ of the soul.

HENRY WADSWORTH LONGFELLOW

For many women, the journey to finding our voice is a living thing.

It is a lengthy thing.

It can be a sacred thing.

We see this in the keening of women down through the ages.

In our laments and in our storytelling.

For some in our protests and, for some, in our prayers.

Standing alone and standing together.

It grows from the burning in our bellies and our belief in a better future.

Our voice is a powerful, purposeful, transformational tool. We are wise to steward its development in ourselves and others with great care.

Think about the astonishing example of how the gift of communication brought freedom and meaning on that miraculous day when teacher Anne Sullivan spelled the word water into the hand of the blind and deaf Helen Keller. Helen wrote later in her diary, "That living word awakened my soul, gave it light, hope, joy, set it free… I saw everything with the strange new sight that had come to me."

Think of the impact words have on our daily lives through conversation with a friend, catchy ads, great literature, the ability to understand what a 2-year-old wants, hurtful comments, or someone's last words. Words matter. Communication matters. Our Voice includes and also transcends these.

A dear friend responded to her history of domestic violence by creating an art installation of hundreds of wood cutouts of women whose silhouettes were painted black. Each woman represented a woman who had died as a result of domestic violence and held her story. Overnight the tractor-trailer pulled up at the City Hall of cities across the USA and unloaded these standing stories in silence. As people walked through them on their way to and from work the "Silent Witness" spoke much more powerfully than words could have. The next morning the cutouts were gone. Hidden. Like the problem. The message was moving—in both senses of the word.

True voice grows out of our personality and passion. It grows out of our credibility and experiences. It grows out of our convictions, pain and passion. It grows out of our character. It grows out of our values.

True Voice, spoken and otherwise, grows from a place deep within us and informs not only our private and public conversation and but also our priorities and practices.

Yet for many women finding our voice is complicated by many factors. Consider that:

While today's Disney's princesses are a sassier, pluckier bunch [than the early ones] research has found a surprising trend. Even when they have the starring role, women speak only a minority of the dialogue—and far less than they did in the films of the 1930s and '50s. While female characters speak 50% to 70% of the lines in the vintage movies Cinderella, Sleeping Beauty, and Snow White and the Seven Dwarfs, those in subsequent films are lucky to get even one-third of the dialogue… In Mulan, whose titular heroine has saved China by the time the credits roll, females speak 23% of the dialogue… Even Frozen, the mega-blockbuster starring two princess sisters, gives women only 41% of the dialogue. The only exceptions to the female-minority rule are Tangled and Brave, whose female characters speak 52% and 74% of the lines.[88] Mulan has a female lead but Mushu, her male protector dragon speaks 50% more than she does.[89]

This phenomenon is not only true of Disney movies. New York Times film critic Kevin B. Lee found that Best Actor nominees for the Academy Awards spent an average of 85 minutes onscreen in their films, compared to 57 minutes for Best Actress nominees.[90] Even movies with strong female leads like *Pretty Woman* have more male voices speaking than female. Romantic comedies have dialogue that is on average 58% male. And while the percentage of male voices increases with age the percentage of aging female voices decreases drastically.[91]

Reflect: What insights and concerns does this raise for you?

Reflect: Has this been your experience? Do the young women on your team speak up as much as the men do? Why or why not?

No wonder so many women struggle with using their voice. The author of *How Remarkable Women Lead*, was asked, "What was the most common obstacle the highly successful businesswomen in her study had to overcome?" She answered, "More than 60 per cent of the women said they didn't naturally have the confidence to speak up for themselves early in their career."[92] And this study was done with highly competent and successful women!

While voice involves more than just speaking, it does include it. Interestingly, "studies repeatedly, but not always consistently, find that it is men who do the talking and women who do the listening…That the actual behavior of the two sexes can be so discrepant from the stereotype is puzzling."[93]

Traditionally, many factors have impacted women's sense of not having a voice. Research shows that girls and women have more difficulty than men in asserting their authority or considering themselves as authorities;[94] in expressing themselves in public so that others will listen;[95] in gaining the respect of others for their minds and their ideas;[96] and in fully utilizing their capabilities and training in the world of work.[97] "In everyday and professional life, as well as in the classroom, women often feel unheard even when they believe they have something important to say."[98]

This may be complicated by a woman's belief that if she develops her powers it will be at the expense of others; that if she excels others may be penalized; or that she should be selfless.[99] Sadly, research demonstrates[100] that girls will often sacrifice their own voice for the sake of saving relationships with their friends.[101] In fact, many girls choose not to become leaders because they fear making decisions, having ideas that are different from their friends, or appearing too achievement-oriented... unfortunately, many girls feel pressured to choose between relationships and leadership.[102]

Even for adult women, various factors may be at work. "Maybe that reluctance to speak masks deeper fears, such as the fear of being 'found out', the fear of being ridiculed, or the fear of being found unworthy… fear drives many women to set an unrealistically high bar that would stop anyone… others confuse respect with remaining silent."[103] No wonder that, when we compare the average woman's self-perception of her boldness in a conversation against other people's, most women gauge their presence as more forceful than others do.[104]

Reflect: Does fear play a role in your willingness to speak up? If so, how has this affected or limited you? If not, what inner belief has protected you from this?

Socialized to be quiet, and then penalized for it, it's no wonder so many women struggle to find their voice.

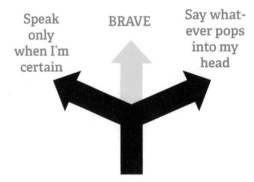

Speak only when I'm certain

BRAVE

Say whatever pops into my head

James R. Detert and others' work[105] on voiceless-ness suggests that a significant portion of someone's sense of voice is predetermined by our previous experiences, often at an early age.[106] This is one reason why many of us, sitting around a decision-making table will struggle to speak up. Remember the freight trains of messages and beliefs we, often unknowingly, pull behind us? These influence our sense of self, willingness to articulate our perspective, and courage to make decisions that will impact ourselves and others.

It is a sobering thought that silence and powerlessness are linked. We cannot think about leadership, social justice, or voice without considering the issue of power. While we often see power as a negative thing, associated with its abuse, its original French root means simply, "to be able." It is only as we reframe power as something helpful, authentic and life-giving that it can be fully embraced. Defining power as energy and strength, something to be taught and shared, seen in relational terms with attributes like collaboration and confidence, rather than domination and control, can completely reframe our perspective. The use and abuse of power has interested me for years. Few things are more pervasive and less openly discussed. From the interaction you may have had with a 2-year-old this morning about brushing their teeth to a teenager out past curfew, to the discussion over who gets the remote or office or budget—issues of power are everywhere.

A voice is a human gift; it should be cherished and used to utter fully human speech as possible. Powerlessness and silence go together.

Margaret Atwood

Reflect: What has been your experience of your own and other's view of power?

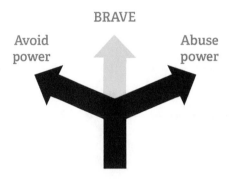

BRAVE

Avoid
power

Abuse
power

How comfortable are you with the concept of personal power? What experiences and messages have helped to craft your view of power and the kind of power you wish to exert?

Catherine the Great of Russia was no stranger to power and intrigue. She ruled after a conspiracy deposed her husband, Peter III. However, Catherine understood power differently from her peers. She once said: "Power without a nation's confidence is nothing." It is one thing to develop our own confidence and another to build others' confidence in us. Both are needed if we are to see transformational change.

Reflect on the quote above. Do you agree? If so how might this principle apply to you?

Tools for Cultivating Our Voice

THE MIXED MESSAGES, high expectations and subsequent low confidence of many women translate into what many psychologists refer to as a global loss of voice. This is worrying on so many levels. The negative impact can hardly be calculated. It spans personal, organizational, community and global levels. We are going to have to go off the beaten track to explore the deep cultural and individual psyche that drives this phenomenon. I promised this journey would take us to some wild places.

This is one of them. We begin by returning to the power of storytelling.

The story of the Selkie's New Skin offers a symbolic representation of the loss of our authentic self. It also speaks to our freedom to seek transformation and the kind of journey that may require. I first read it in Inuit stories and was amazed to find that there are also Welsh, Irish and Scottish versions—some harsher than others. This is one of the gentler versions.

This story takes place on an island at the end of the world—the one you have seen somewhere in your dreams, where the sky is blue, the air is still, the seas are stormy and the coves rocky. Here the wind blows hard and long through the long dark days of winter and summer is fleeting and precious. The island's beaches are filled with seals. Not ordinary seals: they're Selkies. One night every month, it is said they take on human form, stripping off their sealskins and dancing in the moonlight on the beach.

One night a handsome fisherman with coal-black hair and bright blue eyes was feeling restless so he went down to the shore. The sky was midnight-blue velvet as he stared out at the waves. Walking softly he saw a small group of women laughing and calling to each other as they played in the shallow water. These women personified the beauty and mystery of the sea. He wanted one for his wife so he crept up to the rock where they had left their sealskins and took one of the pelts.

After a while the women came back, one by one, put on their sealskins and disappeared into the waves. The last woman searched high and low for her sealskin as her friends called to her. Seeing her distress the man stepped out from where he was hiding and explained that he wished to marry her. He promised to treat her with respect and to give her the choice to return to the sea at the end of seven years. The seal woman shrank from him but eventually realized she had no choice. Reluctantly, with a final look over her shoulder at her sisters and the sea, she went with him. He proved to be a kind and thoughtful husband. Together they built a home and had a daughter whom they named Mara—after the sea.

The young child was at home in her skin. But so had her mother been when she was her age.

The seal woman tried her best to care for her family and to learn to love the land, but as time went on her yearning for her skin increased. She often searched for it at night. When seven years was up she asked for her sealskin back but her husband refused to give it to her.

Mara worried about her mother as she watched her fade away. At night Mara began to drag her mother to the sea to lie in the shallows. She began to secretly search for her mother's sealskin when she became too weak to look herself. Finally, Mara found it hidden under a heap of fraying rope. As she gently picked it up it began to disintegrate in her hands. Being unused for so long it could not be used again.

The seal woman took to her bed and stayed there for weeks on end. The wise old woman who lived in a small stone cottage at the far end of the village said, "Your mother must help herself." So Mara told her mother she must find both the endurance to make the journey to the most westernmost edge of the island and the courage to enter the dark cave of the Old Woman of the World who could be found there. The seal woman protested that she could not possibly undertake this quest but Mara pleaded and wept until her mother could bear her daughter's distress no longer. Rising from her bed she wrapped herself in a cloak and began to walk, clambering in the rain over rocks so slippery that she fell over and over again. At night she cowered in coves. She ate seaweed and drank from icy burns.

One wild day the wind whipped her cloak away and she fell to her knees in despair. Forehead to the ground she felt rather than heard a shuddering rumble in the ground and a woman singing deep below. It seemed to her to be the noise of a spinning wheel pedalled furiously by someone skilled in the art.

Looking all around she found a set of steep stairs, and drawing a deep breath, took the first step down. Carefully down the narrow, slippery steps, she went. Down and down and down. At the bottom the Old Woman sat spinning a fine thread shining with all the colours that ever existed on a rich golden wooden wheel in front of an enormous frame on which was displayed the most beautiful weaving that had ever been created, fringed with sea urchin quills.

"So you have come to find your skin," the Old Woman said. The seal woman nodded yes, teeth chattering from the cold and effort. At the back of the cave was an enormous cauldron which bubbled and steamed releasing the scent of all the seeds and herbs and growing things in the world. As she sat and ate the warmth came back into the seal woman's bones and she listened as the Old Woman spoke.

"Your old skin is of no use. I'd heard all the stories of Selkies who find their old skins and swim off as if nothing has ever happened. And maybe that happens sometimes but often it doesn't. And sometimes it shouldn't." The Old Woman handed her a cup of something hot and sweet. She took and sipped it gratefully. Strength began to flood back into her soul.

"You've done well to make it this far, Daughter," the Old Woman said. "But there is more to do before you're done." And she told the Selkie what she must do.

The sea was calm and the air still when she set off again. She found a curragh at the base of the cliff just where the Old Woman had said she would. Climbing in she rowed slowly across to the tiny island a mile to the north and a mile to the west. She brought the curragh to rest on a long white strand in a sandy cove and found the cave the Old Woman had told her about. She reached for the skin she found there, held it to her breast, smelled the scent of home and slipped it on.

It would have been easy for her to go then, following her seal sisters home. But there was more to do before she was done so she slipped off the skin, tucked it in the belt at her waist, picked up the oars and began her long return.

She came to Mara while her husband was away fishing. Taking her to the shore, she taught her all she needed to know. She taught her a song she could sing to call the Selkie to her anytime she wished so they could meet again and again at the shore. She also taught her the song that would sing her soul back home.

Reflect: How do you respond to this story?

In this story "the Selkie's skin is the source of her life-giving, creative power, ...that smelt so wonderfully of home and of herself, in all her natural wildness."[107] It is also the source of her courage and uniqueness. It represents the value of being rooted in heritage and habitat. For many years the seal woman did not realize the consequences of her loss. Once understood, the call to return was powerful. Sadly her old skin no longer served her well. It had disintegrated through disuse so she had to find another way. She had to help herself. This took a monumental effort as she had grown weary and jaded.[108]

"We [too] may need to travel a long way to find the new skin that fits us, and before we can learn to be comfortable in it—but first we must commit ourselves to the journey."[109]

Reflect: In what ways are you excited about the journey of life and the self-discovery it allows?

Joseph Campbell has popularized the epic quest, the Hero's journey… but for many women, our journey "resembles a pilgrimage more than an adventure…. a search for becoming."[110]

The Selkie was not given a map for her journey and neither are we. She is given a starting point. With this first step and a wise companion, she returns to the place of her belonging and explores the spaces of her own becoming.

Reflect: In what ways, if any, do you relate to this story?

Reflect: We also may have skins that have been stolen or, more often, that we hide away. Do you sense that you have any false skin(s) that are no longer fitting you?

What is your song of yearning for a part of you that has been lost?

Old women are common figures in archetypal stories. These elders may be patient or feisty, loud or quiet. They rarely hold positions of power and yet are seen by others as very powerful. This is due to their moral courage, ability to gather people together and counter-cultural worldview. Jungian psychologist Marion Woodman defines the most iconic image of elder women—the Crone—as "alarmingly present. Like a tuning fork, her truth shatters hypocrisy. Others in her presence are released into what is true in themselves. Or flee."[111] Don't you love that image of a tuning fork?

Reflect: Who or what are your "old women"?

In what ways are the wise women in your life alarmingly present and how do they enable you to shatter hypocrisy?

In many Native American cultures, Councils of Grandmothers and Clan Mothers were regularly consulted before major decisions were made. In Celtic cultures and stories, elder women guarded the health of the community and the balance of the natural world. How do the wise women in your life protect you? How do they guard the community, belong to their places and speak into the balance of the natural world?

Reflect: Where or what are your caves?

What cauldrons of nourishment and transformation have you experienced?

163

Reflect: Who, what or where is your sea? Your element? Your home place? The Welsh have a word for our deep longing for home: *hiraeth*. While not all cultures have as powerful a word many of us share a similar longing.

Reflect: What stories have you been told that are shaping you in life-giving ways?

Reflect: Weaving is a common theme in ancient stories written by women about women. What do you think the weaving in the story represents? Why might the wise woman be spinning and weaving? Might there be any significance to the fact that it can be heard through the rock?

What stories have you had to unweave from your own because they were destructive (e.g. the only way to belong is to conform)?

A contemporary example by textile artist Candice Ball of Way Through the Wilderness Handwovens

Women's journeys, especially our internal journeys, are rarely linear. Often we circle back to similar themes or issues various times throughout our lives. Do not be discouraged by this. Each circle represents the opportunity to go a bit deeper. This is especially true for pilgrimages.

Reflect: What themes seem to surface again and again for you?

Reflect: Where have you experienced (or longed for) pilgrimage? What is it you crave?

Our true voice grows from within. It requires wisdom and courage. It transforms us even as it creates opportunities to transform our world.

Reflect on the following:

"Wisdom and courage are lovers.
Their secret is that their dwelling has no lamps.
At sunset they say a prayer that in the night
their ears, noses, tongues
Will tell them what they need to know.

At sunrise they say another prayer;
That their vision will not depend
merely on what the daylight reveals.

The neighbors find them odd,
But their children –
Compassion, Integrity, and Hope –
Have learned the wonder of a heart un-hiding itself,
Coming as gift to our deepest eye."[112]

Reflect: Do you agree that compassion, integrity and hope are born of a heart that has unhidden itself?

Reflect: How is your journey shaping your voice?

It is not overstating it to say a strong voice is impossible without a strong character. Perhaps no character trait is more critical for BRAVE influencers than Moral Courage. Moral courage involves the desire, will, and ability to do what is right even when there is a cost.

BRAVE women make self-respect their goal, not popularity.

Ohio State University psychologist Jennifer Crocker found that people who base their self worth on what others think, pay both a mental and physical price. Those who depend on others' approval are more likely to experience higher levels of stress, drug abuse and eating disorders. People who base their self-esteem on internal sources such as a strong moral code are not only less likely to exhibit these negative symptoms but they also do better academically.[113]

The word integrity comes from a root word meaning wholeness. We use it here meaning both our wholeness and the more common understanding of our honesty. One of my favorite ways of thinking about this is through exploring the original meaning of the word sincerity.

Our grandparents grew up knowing that when they signed a letter "sincerely yours," it had meaning. However, we have lost both the art of letter writing and the understanding of what sincerity truly means. In Roman times, disreputable potters were known to fill cracks in their pots with wax before glazing them. Unsuspecting purchasers would only discover the flaw when the pot was heated. More reputable potters began to hang signs claiming their pots were *sincerus*—meaning "without wax." To end a letter with "sincerely" was, therefore, to sign one's name to the veracity of all that was written above.

169

> Credibility is not dependent on perfection, but it is dependent on sincerity.

Imagine taking the time to reflect on every document, conversation and proposal to be able to, with integrity, attach our signature and our reputation to it.

A dear potter friend, Cal MacFarlane, once led us through a powerful exercise that modelled this in a memorable way. It was one of those dark, crisp Canadian winter nights when icicles began to form on our eyebrows and even through thick scarves, our breaths were visible as steam. Earlier we had written regrets, mistakes and weaknesses on scraps of paper and dropped them into our unbaked glazed pots.

Now Cal, clad in a parka and elbow-high heat-resistant gloves, picked up each pot with giant tongs and placed it carefully into the jet-engine-looking fiery red kiln. Then lifting the lid in an act of pure theatre, he plunged the hot pots into dry pine needles firing sparks and smoke into the jet-black air. Still gasping we watched as these same pots were plunged into cold water, crystals of ice melting as the hot pots sizzled. Every sense was awakened with the sights, sounds and smells of the experience. We assumed our papers had burned away in the process, but Cal explained they had not. They had been assimilated into the pots—now part of the crackle of the fragile yet beautiful raku fired pots. It is a picture of how the crucible of life transforms our imperfections. They have not burned away; they become part of us. They add to our beauty and our vulnerability. They are part of who we are, and they are an important piece of what enables us to do what we long to do.

Reflect: What belongs on your scrap of paper? How is the furnace of your life journey assimilating your regrets, mistakes and weaknesses into the fabric of who you are in ways that enables you to be both more beautiful and more vulnerable?

We can take this metaphor a step further by considering the Japanese art of *kintsukuroi*. In this tradition, breakage and repair were considered part of a piece's rich history, not a reason to be discarded, or a fact to be hidden. Pots with cracks were understood to have endured great heat and pressure and were therefore treated with great care. The cracks were filled with gold and lacquer, such that the pot was even stronger and more beautiful. The cracks were celebrated and enhanced. The journey of the pot—both through hard knocks and gentle care—was honoured.

Our voice grows out of the solid, noble, whole, and compassionate parts of our lives. However, it also includes the brokenness, the cracks, the wax, the drama, and the genuine trauma. BRAVE leaders learn to use appropriate vulnerability as well as stories of victory and perseverance to tell our stories in ways that mend ourselves and provide hope and meaning for others.

Reflect: How is your life journey enabling you to see the cracks as beautiful? How might these very areas become some of the strongest parts of who you are and what you have to offer?

As Dr. Brené Brown suggests, "Have the courage to be imperfect… Let go of who you think you should be, to be who you are. Fully embrace vulnerability, because what makes you vulnerable also makes you beautiful."

Personal Exercise: Draw a simple pottery shape, carefully considering what shape it should be—an open bowl, a tapered vase, a cup or chalice? Add words, images or lines to present any known cracks. Reflect on how you have sought to hide these or allowed them to become places of greater strength and beauty. In what ways does this exercise cause you to look at your voice differently?

Strong voices are as diverse as we are but they share certain traits in common. Perhaps the most powerful one is the fire within. Conviction. Where does this motivating force, this burning desire to change something come from? For some, it is an innate sensitivity to right and wrong. For many of us, it grows from experience. When the pain we have experienced ourselves, or seen in others, collides with the passions we long to see at work in our world its sparks a fire. This fire may start small and build, or it may flare up quickly and unexpectedly. No matter. The fire is there for a reason. Learn to use it wisely. Do not use it to burn others. Do not let it consume you. Ration it out with caution so as not to allow it to burn out. The Ancient Mothers spoke of a furnace that must be tended. They warned against opening the door too often or too wide lest the fire go out. Learn to fan the flame when needed so as to ensure we do not become cold.

Reflect: What "fire" burns within you and how do you protect it from growing too hot or too cold?

Values Exercises: A powerful way to uncover our true values (the principles that drive our actual behaviour) is to ask friends to share what they see in you. This can often lead to great insights.

Another way is to think about the people you most admire. What is it that you admire about them and is this because this is a high value to you?

Another powerful exercise involves gathering a small group and telling them the story of a time that really mattered to you and where you felt you were "at your best." Ask them to listen without interrupting and to jot down any values that they hear while you are talking. Record what others share and reflect on them. Where do you agree? Disagree? What do they show you about yourself? What do your values cause you to do? Cause you not to do?

Our voice carries considerable weight because of both the truth of the message and the credibility of the messenger. Credibility includes our reputation but goes beyond this to include that elusive "in a world saturated with messages[,] why should I listen to you?" quality. While several factors contribute to this credibility, a few stand out as critical.

1. Have we lived it? Do we understand some of the nuances, or are we reflecting as an uninformed outsider? For example, we don't have to have lived in poverty to help address it, but we had better have some people on our team who have.
2. Have we got an idea that is worth trying? Ranting about injustice and bringing a fresh idea that just might work are two very different approaches that lead to very different outcomes.
3. Are we doing something about this ourselves? What kind of commitment and sacrifice are we making before we ask others to do the same?

Reflect: What idea do you have that is worth trying and that you are personally invested in? If you were to start (or restart with fresh inspiration and direction) doing something about this idea, what would the next steps be?

We may not know how to find our full voice, but we know it when we see it. I met Alice when attending some NGO meetings at the UN Commission on the Status of Women in Manhattan. She was delightful. Standing shoulder high to the rest of us, Alice was soft-spoken, compassionate, inclusive and humorous—the perfect grandmother figure. Later that day, in a large group meeting, I heard someone stand behind me to address what the panel had just said. Turning to see who it was, I was floored to see my new friend Alice. The tiny granny transformed into a lioness as she spoke with clarity and authority. I had to bite my lip to keep from laughing with joy. When Alice stood, eighty years of advocacy and action rose with her. When she spoke, it was with the voice of one who had both earned the right and had something important to say. I don't know at what point Alice found her informed, seasoned voice, but on that day I trembled knowing I had heard something majestic. Not surprisingly, the whole room listened. There was a palpable energy that bounced back and forth across the room for a full, silent moment after she sat down. A lioness had just roared. And we all knew it.

Reflect: What is your lioness longing to roar?

Studies indicate that women, when starting in their vocation, hold back because they do not feel they have anything important to say, or believe that, since they are in a junior position, it is not their place to insist that their viewpoint be heard. However, many senior leaders told of a breakthrough moment, in which either holding back led to a failure, or contributing led to a success. From then on, they made a conscious decision to make their voice heard—and to insist that others they lead speak up as well.[114]

Reflect: The words vocation and voice come from the same Latin root, *vocare*, which means "calling." How does this cause you to think differently about your voice? About your vocation?

Voice is often affirmed in community. It is developed through a complex and individualized pathway involving our own courage and determination and the feedback and opportunities offered by those whom we perceive as truth-tellers and gatekeepers.

Reflect: How has your community affirmed your voice? How has it suppressed it?

Ko taku reo taku ohooho,
ko taku reo taku māpihi mauria.

My language is my awakening,
my language is the window to my soul.

MAORI PROVERB

Reflect: How has your voice caused an awakening within you or others?

My favourite description of voice is "threading instinct and experience into the fulcrum of sharp, clear expression. Born at the intersection of tentativity [*sic*] and certainty, it requires both vulnerability and presence...leaders need to find their own voices... to have voice is to be fully present, to feel counted in, and counted on, to have something to say, and to be heard."[115]

Reflect: I love the way this quote plays with the tensions of vulnerability and certainty. It speaks to having something to say and the importance of being heard. And it links belonging, contribution and voice. What do you like (or dislike) about this description? What does it suggest to you about your voice? How is voice connected to presence?

The Matters to Me Voice is directive and assertive. It advocates well but may not listen well. There are times this voice is needed, but its excessive use may indicate self-serving advocacy.

The Gives Life to Me Voice is compassionate to self. It understands her own needs and preferences. While our true Voice will not always be so kind to self, we will burn out if we neglect this part of our message for too long.

The Matters to Others Voice listens well but does not advocate. It tends to minimize its own perspective and may be passive or avoidant. Like any of the Voices, it has a powerful place when used in healthy ways but can quickly undermine one's confidence and impact if misused.

The Gives Life to Others Voice is compassionate to others and seeks to understand others' needs and preferences.

Eleanor Roosevelt, mother of five children, wife and political aide to American president F.D. Roosevelt, was also a well-known author, speaker, and activist who helped draft the 1948 UN Declaration of Human Rights. She once said: "Great minds discuss ideas; Average minds discuss events; Small minds discuss people." Choose well what you dedicate your voice to!

One tool that may be helpful as we think about developing our distinctive voice is the Life-Giving Voice Model.

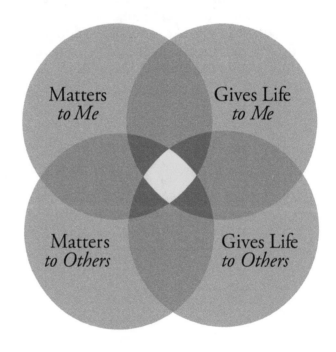

The four quadrants represent four foci. In the sweet spot where these overlap a truly powerful and sustainable Life Giving Voice is found.

When we are advocating strongly for our opinions and seeking input, aware of our own and others' needs and preferences, we are practicing a Life Giving Voice. This more readily enables us to seek a creative, wise and sustainable third way;   A BRAVE way.

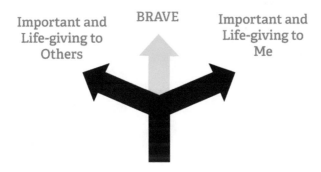

Important and
Life-giving to
Others

BRAVE

Important and
Life-giving to
Me

Reflect: Which quadrants do you tend to hang out in? Why is this?

Reflect: What benefits can you see from developing and utilizing all four? What steps would enable you to move towards that sweet spot?

BRAVE Leaders embrace Balance, Bright minds, unique Beauty, and Boldness. They seek the gift of Resilience born of hope. They learn to Act and Advocate according to their passions and strengths in service of the world's true needs. They cultivate their life-giving, proactive Voice. Yet one thing remains. We must be open to Expand our perspective and influence. It is to this critical part of our journey that we travel next.

BRAVE:

Expanded Perspective and Influence

ONE DAY A YOUNG WOMAN WE WILL CALL ANNA participated in a leadership program in the Leadership Studio where I work. She sat in the back row, rarely raising her eyes, let alone her voice. Becoming increasingly concerned that we were not reaching this young woman, we sought to balance inviting her participation with respecting the discomfort she obviously felt when called on in any way. After three rounds of a three-day program, I worried we were adding to rather than relieving her angst. In the debriefing circle at the end of the final retreat, I was wracking my brain to try to figure out how to allow her to contribute without embarrassing her. To our great surprise, she volunteered a response. Her words were penetratingly profound.

She said, "I still don't think of myself as a leader. But I have begun to realize that if I did, I would look at the whole world differently, and that would change everything for me and maybe for others around me as well."

Twenty-four normally rambunctious, students sat in the sacred silence of that moment; looking at her with both compassion and respect. It was as if she had spoken on behalf of thousands of us around the world.

Many women struggle with calling themselves leaders for all the reasons we have addressed above. Yet leadership is really about becoming the best version of ourselves and using our influence to make the world a better place.

Reflect: How would you describe your leadership confidence?

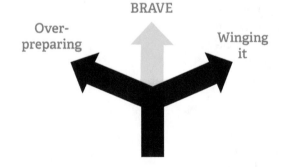

While some people may more naturally gravitate towards leadership, we can all practice leadership mindsets and behaviours.

The first step is to acknowledge that we look at the world through a deeply ingrained lens that both illuminate and distort reality. Even those who have travelled, read and experimented widely encounter this. One lens can never offer the ever-changing beauty and complexity of the full kaleidoscope we need to truly see. There are at least three places we will need to look to expand our perspective.

> Looking in—at what is changing within us
> Looking around—at what is really going on
> Looking forward—at what could be

Looking inward through Self Reflection and Experimentation

"Everyone thinks of changing the world, but no one thinks of changing [the]mself."
Count Leo Tolstoy, Russian novelist (1828-1910)

It really is true that we must "be the change we long to see." If we are going to become the kind of BRAVE women our world so desperately needs, the transformation must begin in us.

Sadly many bright and beautiful young women are scarred by the messages they heard about their value during junior high and high school. The Tall Poppy Syndrome we mentioned earlier contributes to a fundamental fear of standing out. Snickers and arched eyebrows, expulsion from cliques, de-friending and the retraction of social invitations are incredibly common and destructive for many competent, and even previously well-liked girls.

189

Tall Poppy Syndrome
Smart Girl Syndrome
Bullying
Mean Girls
Impossible standards of body image

It is a wonder and a testimony to our resilience that we survive at all.

There is a strong correlation between the beliefs we have regarding our ability and how we show up to new experiences. This is why our mindset and the stats and stories we tell ourselves are so important. While every step of our journey matters there are critical mindset-developing windows for young women. These often occur at points of transition. The time you take to explore these issues now will help craft your life-long well being and leadership influence.

Why? Young women engage in an inner journey that takes them deep into issues of identity, value, contribution and belonging. This is the season where intentionality is critical. Self-restricting frameworks can be challenged. Unhealthy patterns can be broken. And with our transformation, the Goliaths of the world truly can be brought down.

Mature mentors and coaches help us navigate unknown terrain.

Finding great mentors can seem daunting. The key is setting realistic boundaries. The following guidelines may be helpful.

The people you would love to be coached by are most likely busy people. They may also have others asking them to mentor them. Find ways to make it easy for them to spend time with you. Offer to drive them places. Help them with a project. Come prepared with questions. Take notes. Follow up on any ideas or homework they give you, and let them know you have done so. Mentoring does not have to involve a long-term relationship.

It is amazing what can be accomplished in 4-6 sessions. Finish well by genuinely and appropriately thanking your mentor and asking them to recommend who you could meet with next. This sets you on a path to a whole series of amazing relationships and a powerful network of supporters and wisdom carriers.

Be as intentional about coaching others as you would like others to be about pouring into you. Find someone with potential and invite them to lunch. Include them in the work you are doing and teach them the things you are learning. Learn to ask great questions.

Reflect: Who in your life acts as a coach or mentor for you? Are you accessing them frequently enough? Are you coming prepared and gaining as much as you could from your times together?

Who are you intentionally pouring into? Are you strategic in the way you maximize your time together?

Self-awareness and self-regulation exercises like the ones we have done in this book, can be really helpful. However, these should be balanced by stretch goals to keep us from becoming too internally focused, self-conscious or perfectionist-ic. Sadly, many women get stuck here. Stretch goals enable us to move outside our comfort zone and experiment with new ways of thinking and acting.

Reflect: What personal stretch goals would you like to set?

Reflect: If you were to set a "change the world for the better" stretch goal for yourself what would it be?

For a complex series of reasons, many women find viewing or describing themselves as leaders uncomfortable. This is understandable but unfortunate. A leadership mindset enables the sense of agency we need to affect positive change.

The development of this mindset has important windows at grades 3, 6 through 8, 9 through 12, entering and post-university and after childbearing. Without intentional intervention, many of us will experience our leadership confidence levels dropping. This causes us to self-limit at the very time that the world around us needs us the most.

There is such a high cost to women's low confidence. While sixty-nine percent of young girls (the same percentage as boys) consider themselves leaders, only thirty-six percent are interested in being a leader when they get older.[116] Admittedly not everyone aspires to leadership, as it has been traditionally defined. However, this gap is interesting and prompts the question, "What happened in between?"

Reflect: What self-awareness, skills building and leadership development experiences did you have as a girl? You may need to think beyond traditional or formal opportunities.

How do these influence the way you think about yourself now? How do they influence your belief in your ability to influence the world?

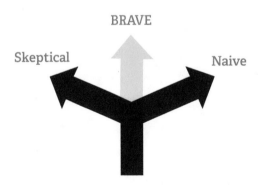

Change comes with daring to dream that something can be better. Transformational change comes from new ways of thinking that lead to new ways of acting and often involves a crucible experience.

In fact, crucible experiences are part of almost every epic quest.

Our daughter recently took up blacksmithing. There is something incredibly empowering about transforming basic metal into works of art by plunging it into a fiery furnace and then pounding and twisting the red hot metal. Without the process of heating, cooling, pounding, bending and shaping, the finished product will shatter when used. It will lack resiliency. There are so many lessons here for us.

A blacksmith learns through apprenticeship. She uses the master's tools and fire to create her own. She learns that first the coal is cooked, turning it into coke, to create the perfect cauldron culture for transformation to occur. Then the steel is held in the hottest part of the fire until it passes through the various shades of colour that represent its own chemical transformation. Finally, it is ready for shaping. The master uses heavier tools and fewer strikes. The apprentice takes longer, making multiple important mistakes along the way as they learn. If they follow the process and practice regularly, eventually their pieces will be strong, flexible, useful and beautiful.

I have learned so many lessons from watching this mesmerizing process:

- A transformational culture is as important as the individual. We used to think that if we transform enough people, it will transform the culture. Now we know that the opposite is true. Be wise about the cultures you immerse yourself in and work hard to create cultures where positive transformation is supported.

- There will be sparks, burns and missteps along the way. Stock up on bandaids. Expect some start-overs. Cut your losses and begin again.
- You will get dirty. Don't worry about the kind of dirt that washes off—you can clean up later—stay focused. Do worry about the kind of dirt that won't wash off. Never sacrifice your values for expediency or people-pleasing.
- The most ordinary of metals can become strong and stunning through transformation.
- Apprenticeship is a tried and true process for development. Look for those who will help you make and learn to use your own tools rather than insist you do things their way.
- The goal of transformation is not self-fulfilment, perfection or people-pleasing. The goal of transformation is purity, strength and usefulness.

Reflect: How does the analogy of blacksmithing inform your thinking regarding your own journey of transformation?

How does it speak to the kind of culture you want to create for yourself and others?

Brittle metal has limited uses. So do brittle people. Coming through the heat both strengthens and softens us, burning off self-righteousness, and building in true compassion for self and others. Coming through the heat changes us from the inside out, altering our motives, strengthening our backbone and making us BRAVE.

It has been said there are two kinds of people. Those who think they can change and those who think they cannot. And that both are right.

Reflect: Where might you have become stagnant in your thinking? What experience or relationship might enable you to break out of this?

Our epic quest travelled wisely, enables us to develop the healthy internal moral code and a strong sense of personal identity needed. Without this, we may overextend, look to others to define us, listen to public opinion regarding what is worth fighting for, allow others to become too dependent on us, or any number of other dangers.

Reflect: Where do you go to strengthen your moral courage and healthy self?

What are the indicators that you are in a good place ethically, emotionally, and spiritually?

Looking out through Expanded Noticing

This is the most basic of skills and yet one of the most difficult. Our worldview creates a set of lenses through which we, often unknowingly, view everything else. As a result, we look without seeing and listen without hearing.

He rangi tā Matawhāiti,
he rangi tā Matawhānui.

The person with a narrow vision sees a narrow horizon,
The person with a wide vision sees a wide horizon.

Maori Proverb

Exercise: Take a walk with eyes, ears, nose, and mind wide open. What do you observe? If you were more consciously observant, in what ways might it influence your life?

Exercise: Sit in a coffee shop or your company lunchroom with your computer open to a blank screen, to appear to be working but not be distracted. Listen to the conversations around you. What do they tell you about what matters to human beings? How might you apply these insights to the questions you are asking and the obstacles you are facing?

Reflect: In what ways is the ability to truly see what is going on important to your life and work right now?

What are you doing to hone your noticing skills?

The next step in expanding our perspective comes through developing the art of asking great questions. This is a fun and powerful tool that can take us, and others, down completely different trajectories of thought and action. What if no one had ever asked, "I wonder if it is possible to get to the moon?" or "How could we talk to people on the other side of the world?" Great questions start with genuine curiosity. They steer us away from, "Whose fault is it?" and towards, "How can we think about this differently?" Great questions help us dig deeper and deeper until we get to the root of something while pushing us further and further outwards towards the periphery of untested possibility.[117]

Reflect: What ten questions have you never asked that are worth asking? Who are the right people to get in the room to discuss them with?

Reflect: What paradigm shifting question are you wishing someone would ask you?

What is stopping you from crafting and reflecting on your own breakthrough questions?

Looking forward at what is possible through Visioning and Collaboration

Leaders are constantly framing both current reality and future vision. This is important for our team. It is equally important to us. It builds our BRAVE. Anna Fels, interviewing young women for a book on women's ambition, discovered that "the liveliness and pleasure with which [they] told their stories often corresponded closely to their level of self-esteem and general sense of well-being."[118] Women who had a dream were more likely to be confident and animated. That is insightful, don't you think? If we are growing weary, complacent or discouraged, perhaps our vision needs a boost.

Reflect: What are you dreaming that you have not dared to share with anyone yet?

Reflect: What do you need to do to re-inspire yourself?

Marcel Proust once said:
"The real journey of discovery consists not in seeking new landscapes, but having new eyes."

Reflect: How might a fresh set of lenses help you to see in ways that would enable you to be more BRAVE? Where do you need to go to get those lenses?

Provocative questions such as the following might be helpful as a part of the visioning process:

- How important is this? Why?
- What kind of obstacles might we encounter? Will it be worth finding a way around them?
- What processes will we use in finding a way?
- How can we ensure we build towards both transformational results and transformed relationships?
- What first steps could be taken to test a theory or shorten the gap?
- What is already being done, that could be leveraged for greater breakthrough or sustainability?
- How could we be even more intentionally inclusive?
- What could we approach this with greater wisdom and innovation?

What other questions would you like to add?

"To dare is to lose one's footing momentarily.
Not to dare is to lose oneself."
SOREN KIRKEGAARD

Any dream worth dedicating your life to will normally involve other people. However, inviting others in comes at a cost. Things may move slower. Differences of opinion arise, and time is spent resolving these. More conversations are needed, and decisions are not made as quickly. Then, one glorious day you hear someone talking about what we do, what we believe, what we have accomplished and it strikes you that not only could you not have done this alone but that the journey has been sweeter and stronger with others. In the process, you will find that you have grown so much more. The project has gone places you could never have taken it and will carry on after you are gone.

Reflect: What partnerships would enable your initiative to take off if they could be built with trust and integrity?

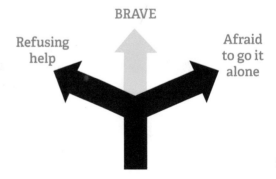

BRAVE

Refusing
help

Afraid
to go it
alone

Trust is the currency of transformational relationships.

It is a byproduct of three R's:
Respect + Relationship + Results = Trust

- Respect is earned through the consistent demonstration of character, values, acknowledging when we have made mistakes and wisdom.
- Relationships take time to build and involve a genuine commitment to the best interests of others.
- Results must match the expectations of others to build trust.

The three R's interact. To build trust, all three must be consistently demonstrated. No wonder that, without a proven track record, it is difficult to build trust. Even with a history of results ,we can quickly lose the trust of those who doubt our commitment to them. Have you ever noticed that while we tend to judge ourselves according to our intentions, we truly do judge others according to their behaviour? Good intentions are actually not enough. We must demonstrate our commitment in ways that align with the way others can best receive it.

The quickest way to lose trust is to say one thing and do another—or say one thing to one person and something else to someone else. Nowhere is this more pronounced than in those working on behalf of the marginalized where trust is a rare and often abused commodity.

Reflect: Which of the three R's would others give you the highest ranking on? What behaviours might you begin practicing that could make you even more trustworthy (without becoming unhealthily dependent on others' approval) in your decision-making?

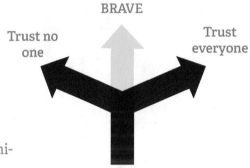

BRAVE

Trust no one

Trust everyone

How skilled are you at assessing the trustworthiness of others?

What mindsets or behaviours need to change for you to move forward in transformative ways?

Where Will Your BRAVE Take You?

WE BEGAN OUR JOURNEY TOGETHER with the dirt beneath our feet—the rich humus that teams with organic and inorganic complexity. True Bravery is embedded in humility. Humility lies not in self-abasement or the inaction born of self-doubt. It is found most readily as we truly enter into the beauty and brokenness of our world, of ourselves and of those around us. To be BRAVE is to celebrate what it means to be fully human and to dare to believe that one imperfect person, or better yet a small group of gloriously imperfect people, can make a difference in their world.

I invite you to choose Bravery. To allow hope to fuel your Resilience when you fall or get knocked down. To Advocate and Act wisely and compassionately for yourself and others. To cultivate your Voice. To Expand your perspective and to help others do the same.

I invite you to pop on those yellow flips flops and get up behind that podium your voice is intended to speak from; to strap on those running shoes and prepare yourself for a few hurdles along the way; to tie tight those hiking boots and go off the beaten path to find another way. All of us grandmas will be cheering you on from the grandstands, countless people's lives will be different because of you, and many kids will be watching to learn how it is done.

Will you mess up? Yes, absolutely. Expect that. Know that you will recover and be stronger afterwards. Know that many hands will be there to help you back up if you have chosen your friends and mentors wisely. Will it be worth it? Yes, absolutely, because

Life is an epic journey. To live it well we must find our way… our Brave way…to where we belong, to our true selves, and to our true calling.

Our world needs us, and some things are worth fighting for.

As we draw to the close of our journey together, I'd like to offer one final reflection exercise that might help to pull it all together for you. Take your time with this and see where it leads you.

Reflection Exercise: Open your journal to a fresh double page. Imagine that the left-hand page represents your life up until now—the good, the bad, and the ugly. The centerline represents this moment in time. The right-hand page represents everything from this moment forward. Using whatever process is most helpful and whatever medium is most inspiring for you, craft a timeline, collage, list, compilation of symbols, or whatever works for you. Begin to fill the left-hand page with the events, relationships, and internal, and external messages that have shaped who you are and how you think. Some may be major, and others may seem quite small, but if they seem significant to you, include them. Now thoughtfully choose which of these messages, patterns, and priorities you want to carry with you into the future.

Consider the insights you have learned from this book. Record these on the right-hand page of the journal leaving room to add whatever other experiences, relationships, beliefs, priorities, etc. that you want to add. Title the right hand side BRAVE. Now dare to dream. What would you like to add? If money and time were no object, how would you make the world a better place? Share what you have done with someone trusted who is close to you, reflect on their questions and insights and add whatever may be helpful.

There is a BRAVE way. Your BRAVE way.

Where will your BRAVE take you today?

Endnotes

Chapter One: Brave

1. Taylor Clark, *Starbucked: A Double-Tall Tale of Caffeine, Commerce, and Culture* (Back Bay Books, 2008), 208-209.

2. Molly Misetich & Alexandra Delis-Abrams, Ph.D. "Your Self Esteem is up to You." http://www.self-growth.com/articles/Abrams1.htm

3. Nicholas D. Kristof and Sheryl WuDunn, *Half the Sky: Turning Oppression into Opportunity for Women Worldwide* (Knopf, 2009), xx, xxi.

4. See for example, this online resource from Opportunity International: www.opportunity.org/media-center/publications/investing-in-women-and-girls/.

5. Nicholas D. Kristof and Sheryl WuDunn, *Half the Sky: Turning Oppression into Opportunity for Women Worldwide* (Knopf, 2009), xxi.

6. Christopher F. Karpowitz, Tali Mendelberg, and Lee Shaker, "Gender inequality in deliberative participation," American Political Science Review 106, no.3 (2012): 533-47.

7. Nicholas D. Kristof and Sheryl WuDunn, *Half the Sky: Turning Oppression into Opportunity for Women Worldwide* (Knopf, 2009), xvii.

8. "Report to Congress from Attorney General John Ashcroft on U.S. Government Efforts to Combat Human Trafficking in Persons in Fiscal Year 2003." United States, Department of Justice. https://www.hsdl.org/?view&did=481892

9. "Summary Report: the Beijing Declaration and Platform for Action Turns 20." UN Women. http://www2.unwomen.org/~/media/headquarters/attachments/sections/library/publications/2015/sg%20report_synthesis-en_web.pdf?v=1&d=20150226T215547

10. "Introduction to the challenges of achieving gender equality." Global Citizen. https://www.globalcitizen.org/en/content/introduction-to-the-challenges-of-achieving-gender/

11. "Invest in Girls' Equality." WomenDeliver.org. http://womendeliver.org/wp-content/uploads/2016/05/Invest_in_Equality_Dec_2015.pdf

12. "Facts & Figures." UN Women. http://www.unwomen.org/en/news/in-focus/commission-on-the-status-of-women-2012/facts-and-figures

13. "International Women's Day: Equality for Women is Progress for all." UNESCO. http://www.unesco.org/new/en/unesco/events/prizes-and-celebrations/celebrations/international-days/international-womens-day-2014/women-ed-facts-and-figure/

14. "Equal access to resources and power for food security in the face of climate change." UN Food and Agriculture Organization. http://www.fao.org/resources/infographics/infographics-details/en/c/180754/

15. "Why many retired women live in poverty." CNN Money. https://money.cnn.com/2014/05/13/retirement/retirement-women/index.html

Chapter Two: BRAVE - Balanced, Bright, Bold, and Beautiful

16. Rachel Simmons, *Enough as She Is: How to Help Girls Move Beyond Impossible Standards of Success to Live Healthy, Happy, and Fulfilling Lives* (HarperCollins, 2018), 174.

17. Researchers found that 5 year old girls were equally likely to think boys and girls could be "really, really smart" but by age 6 they were both absorbing stereotyped notions of boys being smarter and choosing activities based on these stereotypes. ("Gender Stereotypes about intelligence emerge early and influence children's interest," by Lin Bian, Sarah-Jane Leslie and Andrea Cimpian Science, Vol 355, Issue 6323, pages 389-392 Jan 2017. See report at http://science.sciencemag.org/content/355/6323/389)

18. The Organisation for Economic Co-operation and Development 2009 Report on research done in 40 of the world's most developed countries; as quoted in *The Confidence Code*, p. 178,179.

19. Carol Dweck, *Mindset: The New Psychology of Success* (Random House Digital, 2006).

20. Kate Bahn, "Faking It: Women, Academia, and Impostor Syndrome," *Chronicle Vitae*.
https://chroniclevitae.com/news/412-faking-it-women-academia-and-impostor-syndrome

21. See Crandall, Stipek, and Hoffman's work on the negative correlation between intelligence and anticipation of success in young women; quoted in Mary Field Belenky et al, *Women's Ways of Knowing* (Basic Books, 1997), 196.

22. Linda Tarr-Whelan, *Women Lead the Way: Your Guide to Stepping Up to Leadership and Changing the World* (Barrett-Koehler, 2009), 56.

23. Pat Heim and Susan A. Murphy, *In the Company of Women: Indirect Aggression Among Women, Why We Hurt Each Other and How to Stop* (Jeremy P. Tarcher/Putnam, Penguin: 2001), 48.

24. Dove Campaign for Real Beauty

25. Jasna Jovanic et al, "Objective and subjective attractiveness and early adolescent adjustment." *Journal of Adolescence,* 12, issue 2 (June 1989): 225-229.

26. UK GirlGuiding study quoted in *The Guardian,* Sept 2017.

27. According to the National Eating Disorders Association in US.

28. According to DoSomething.org

29. See, for example, Norwegian research by Jorunn Sundgot-Borgen, PhD, and Monica Klungland Torstveit, MS, "Prevalence of Eating Disorders in Elite Athletes Is Higher Than in the General Population," https://www.researchgate.net/publication/8928769_Prevalence_of_Eating_Disorders_in_Elite_Athletes_Is_Higher_Than_in_the_General_Population

30. "Dove, Girls and Beauty Confidence: The Global Report," 2017.

31. Eileen L. Zurbriggen, PhD. "Executive Summary: APA Task Force on the Sexualization of Girls," American Psychological Association, 2007. http://www.apa.org/pi/women/programs/girls/report-summary.pdf

32. Eileen L. Zurbriggen, PhD. "Executive Summary: APA Task Force on the Sexualization of Girls." American Psychological Association, 2007. http://www.apa.org/pi/women/programs/girls/report-summary.pdf

Chapter Three: Enemies of our Confidence

33. Girl Scout Institute, "The State of Girls: Unfinished Business," 56.

34. Rachel Simmons, *Enough as She Is: How to Help Girls Move Beyond Impossible Standards of Success to Live Healthy, Happy, and Fulfilling Lives* (HarperCollins, 2018), x-xi.

35. Rachel Simmons, *Enough as She Is: How to Help Girls Move Beyond Impossible Standards of Success to Live Healthy, Happy, and Fulfilling Lives* (HarperCollins, 2018), xi.

36. Rachel Simmons, *Enough as She Is: How to Help Girls Move Beyond Impossible Standards of Success to Live Healthy, Happy, and Fulfilling Lives* (HarperCollins, 2018), xiv.

37. Avivah Wittenberg-Cox & Alison Maitland, *Why Women Mean Business* (Wiley, 2009), 238.

38. Katty Kay and Claire Shipman, *The Confidence Code* (HarperBusiness, 2014), 16-17.

39. Ernesto Reuben, Columbia University Business School Journal, Ideas at Work: "Confidence Game," as quoted in *The Confidence Code,* 19.

40. Katty Kay and Claire Shipman, *The Confidence Code* (HarperBusiness, 2014), 35.

41. Robin F. Goodman, quoted in Natalia Brzezinski, "Building Our Daughters' Self Esteem, By Starting With Our Own," HuffPost Blog, 2010.

42. Rachel Simmons, *Enough as She Is: How to Help Girls Move Beyond Impossible Standards of Success to Live Healthy, Happy, and Fulfilling Lives* (HarperCollins, 2018), xiii.

43. YPULSE, in partnership with Claire Shipman & Katty Kay, "The Confidence Code for Girls: The Confidence Collapse and Why it Matters for the Next Gen," https://static1.squarespace.com/static/588b93f6b-f629a6bec7a3bd2/t/5ac39193562fa73cd8a07a89/1522766258986/The+Confidence+Code+for+Girls+x+Y-pulse.pdf

44. We will use the words self-esteem, self-efficacy, and confidence interchangeably. Although I realize they have some differences of meaning, in this context of this chapter they express the same concept.

45. Melba Pattillo Beals, *I will not fear: My story of a lifetime of building faith under fire* (Baker, 2018), 123.

46. Adapted from work done by Sue Monk Kidd.

47. Courtney Martin, *Perfect Girls, Starving Daughters* (Berkley, 2008), as quoted in Rachel Simmons, *Enough As She Is*, xii.

48. KPMG. "KPMG Women's Leadership Study." 2015, 10.

49. Rachel Simmons, *Enough as She Is: How to Help Girls Move Beyond Impossible Standards of Success to Live*

Healthy, Happy, and Fulfilling Lives (HarperCollins, 2018), 149.

50. Katty Kay and Claire Shipman, *The Confidence Code: The Science and Art of Self-Assurance—What Women Should Know* (HarperBusiness, 2014), 133.

51. Katty Kay and Claire Shipman, *The Confidence Code: The Science and Art of Self-Assurance—What Women Should Know* (HarperBusiness, 2014), 151-152.

52. See research by Cheryl van Daalen-Smith at York University, *Living as a Chameleon, A Guide to Understanding Girls' Anger for Girl-Serving Professionals*. Or summary article by the Toronto Star on March 2, 2007 called "The Fire Within."

Chapter Four: Tools to Build our Confidence

53. A. Bandura, *Self-Efficacy: The Exercise of Control* (W.H. Freeman, 1997).

54. Ben Okri, *A Way of Being Free* (Orion, 1997), 46.

55. See the rest of the poem and the story of its creation on the author's website: http://www.georgeellalyon.com/where.html

Chapter Five: BRAVE - Resilience

56. Rachel Simmons, *Enough as She Is: How to Help Girls Move Beyond Impossible Standards of Success to Live Healthy, Happy, and Fulfilling Lives* (HarperCollins, 2018), 168.

57. Sharon Blackie, *If Women Rose Rooted: A Journey to Authenticity and Belonging* (September Publishing, 2017), 13.

58. Thomas King, *The Truth About Stories, A Native Narrative* (Anansi, 2003), 95.

Chapter Six: Tools to Develop Our Resilience

59. Sara Rimer. "For Girls, It's Be Yourself, and Be Perfect, Too." NY Times, April 1, 2007. http://www.nytimes.com/2007/04/01/education/01girls.html

60. Marcus Buckingham, *Find Your Strongest Life: What the Happiest and Most Successful Women Do Differently* (Thomas Nelson, 2009), 17-26.

61. Marcus Buckingham, *Find Your Strongest Life: What the Happiest and Most Successful Women Do Differently* (Thomas Nelson, 2009), 17-26.

62. Marcus Buckingham, *Find Your Strongest Life: What the Happiest and Most Successful Women Do Differently* (Thomas Nelson, 2009), 16.

63. Marcus Buckingham, *Find Your Strongest Life: What the Happiest and Most Successful Women Do Differently* (Thomas Nelson, 2009), 89-92.

Chapter Seven: Thriving

64. 6 Ways to Foster Belonging in the Workplace: Taking Diversity & Inclusion to the Next Level, a Culture Amp ebook, 7. http://hello.cultureamp.com/6-ways-to-foster-belonging-in-the-workplace

65. Rachel Simmons, *Enough as She Is: How to Help Girls Move Beyond Impossible Standards of Success to Live Healthy, Happy, and Fulfilling Lives* (HarperCollins, 2018), xvii.

66. J. C. Kennedy, Leadership and Culture in New Zealand, Commerce Division, Lincoln University, quoted in "Leadership in Aotearoa New Zealand: A Cross Cultural Study," by Dale Pfeifer, Massey University and Matene Love, Victoria University, 23.

67. Mandivamba Rukuni, *Leading Afrika* (Penguin Books, 2009), 1, 2.

68. See also, Howard Zehr, *The Little Book of Restorative Justice* (Good Books, 2002), 19-20.

69. Dr. Brené Brown, *Braving the Wilderness* (Random House, 2017), 160.

70. Hyon S. Chu, "New Technology Industry Diversity and Inclusion report, 2017," Culture Amp. http://hello.cultureamp.com/diversity-and-inclusion

71. Hyon S. Chu, "New Technology Industry Diversity and Inclusion report, 2017," Culture Amp. http://hello.cultureamp.com/diversity-and-inclusion

72. Hyon S. Chu, "New Technology Industry Diversity and Inclusion report, 2017," Culture Amp. http://hello.cultureamp.com/diversity-and-inclusion

73. Rachel Simmons, *Enough as She Is: How to Help Girls Move Beyond Impossible Standards of Success to Live Healthy, Happy, and Fulfilling Lives* (HarperCollins, 2018), xviii.

74. Rachel Simmons, *Enough as She Is: How to Help Girls Move Beyond Impossible Standards of Success to Live Healthy, Happy, and Fulfilling Lives* (HarperCollins, 2018), xviii.

75. Higher than divorce, economic, or unemployment rates, according to Jean Twenge, Professor of Psychology, Search Institute research.

76. Ichiro Kawachi and Lisa F. Berkham, "Social ties and mental health," *Journal of Urban Health*, vol. 78, number 3, 2001.

77. Linda Coughlin, Ellen Wingard, Keith Hollihan eds. *Enlightened Power: How Women are Transforming the Practice of Leadership* (Jossey-Bass, 2005), 1.

78. Pat Heim and Susan Murphy, *In the Company of Women: Indirect Aggression Among Women: Why We Hurt Each Other and How to Stop* (TarcherPerigee, 2003), 38-39.

79. Pat Heim and Susan Murphy, *In the Company of Women: Indirect Aggression Among Women: Why We Hurt Each Other and How to Stop* (TarcherPerigee, 2003), 37.

80. Search Institute, "Developmental Relationships Framework." https://www.search-institute.org/developmental-relationships/developmental-relationships-framework/

Chapter Eight: BRAVE - Advocacy and Action

81. John Paul Lederach, *The Little Book of Conflict Transformation* (Good Books, 2003), 20-21.

Chapter Nine: Tools to Practice Advocacy and Action

82. DoSomething.org Campaigns. "11 Facts About Global Poverty." https://www.dosomething.org/us/facts/11-facts-about-global-poverty

83. Maisie Karam, "Trafficking in persons in Canada, 2014," Statistics Canada. https://www150.statcan.gc.ca/n1/pub/85-002-x/2016001/article/14641-eng.htm

84. At the time of writing. "Our Environment," The World Counts. http://www.theworldcounts.com/themes/our_environment

85. "Endangered Species Statistics," Statistic Brain Research Institute, http://www.statisticbrain.com/endangered-species-statistics

86. UN Report on violence against women worldwide, 2015.

Chapter Ten: BRAVE - Voice

87. Friends Committee on National Legislation report, "Prevention is 60:1 Cost Effective," 2011.

88. Corinne Purtill, "Researchers have uncovered a disturbing trend about female characters in Disney movies," Quartz. http://qz.com/603052/new-research-has-uncovered-a-disturbing-trend-about-female-characters-in-disney-movies/

89. Hannah Anderson and Matt Daniels, "Film Dialogue From 2,000 Screenplays Broken Down by Gender and Age," *The Pudding,* https://pudding.cool/2017/03/film-dialogue/

90. Corinne Purtill, "Researchers have uncovered a disturbing trend about female characters in Disney movies," Quartz. http://qz.com/603052/new-research-has-uncovered-a-disturbing-trend-about-female-characters-in-disney-movies/

91. Hannah Anderson and Matt Daniels, "Film Dialogue From 2,000 Screenplays Broken Down by Gender and Age," *The Pudding,* https://pudding.cool/2017/03/film-dialogue/

92. Wallace Immen, "How they managed to rise to the top," The Globe and Mail, Friday, Nov. 13, 2009. http://www.theglobeandmail.com/report-on-business/how-they-managed-to-rise-to-the-top/article1361762/

93. Mary Field Belenky et al., *Women's Ways of Knowing: The Development of Self, Voice and Mind,* 10th ed. (Basic Books, 1997), 45.

94. Clance and Imes 1978: Cross 1968; Macoby and Jacklin 1974; Piliavin 1976; West and Zimmerman 1983 as quoted in Belenky, Clinchy, Goldberger, and Tarule, *Women's Ways of Knowing: The Development of Self, Voice and Mind* (Basic Books, 1997), 5.

95. Aries 1976; Eakins and Eakins1976; Piliavin 1976; Sadker and Sadker 1982;,1985; Swacker 1976;

Thorne 1979 as quoted in Belenky, Clinchy, Goldberger, and Tarule, *Women's Ways of Knowing: The Development of Self, Voice and Mind* (Basic Books, 1997), 5.

96. Hagen and Kahn 1975; Hall and Sandler 1982; Serbin, O'Leary; Kent and Tonick 1973 as quoted in Belenky, Clinchy, Goldberger, and Tarule, *Women's Ways of Knowing: The Development of Self, Voice and Mind* (Basic Books, 1997), 5.

97. Gallese 1985; Kanter 1977; Ruddick and Daniels 1977; Sassen 1980; Treichler and Kramarae 1983 as quoted in Belenky, Clinchy, Goldberger, and Tarule, *Women's Ways of Knowing: The Development of Self, Voice and Mind* (Basic Books, 1997), 5.

98. Mary Field Belenky et al., *Women's Ways of Knowing: The Development of Self, Voice and Mind,* 10th ed. (Basic Books, 1997), 5.

99. Mary Field Belenky et al., *Women's Ways of Knowing: The Development of Self, Voice and Mind,* 10th ed. (Basic Books, 1997), 46.

100. Brown and Gilligan, 1992 as quoted in Girl Scout Research Institute, *Exploring Girls' Leadership: Research Review*, 17. www.girlscouts.org/research

101. Jackson, 2005 as quoted in Girl Scout Research Institute, *Exploring Girls' Leadership: Research Review,* 17. www.girlscouts.org/research

102. Girl Scout Research Institute, *Exploring Girls' Leadership: Research Review,* 17. www.girlscouts.org/research

103. Joanna Barsch and Susie Cranston, *How Remarkable Women Lead* (Crown Business, 2011), 197.136.

104. Joanna Barsch and Susie Cranston, How Remarkable Women Lead (Crown Business, 2011), 197.205.

105. Called "Implicit Voice Theory," the study of beliefs held about ones ability and opportunity to speak up.

106. Jennifer Kish-Gephant, James R. Detert, Linda Klebe Trevino, Amy Edmonston, "Silenced by Fear: The nature, sources, and consequences of fear at work," Research in Organizational Behaviour 29 (2009), 165.

Chapter Eleven: Tools for Cultivating our Voice

107. Sharon Blackie, *If Women Rose Rooted* (September Publishing, 2016), 92.

108. Sharon Blackie, *If Women Rose Rooted* (September Publishing, 2016), 92.

109. Sharon Blackie, *If Women Rose Rooted* (September Publishing, 2016), 92.

110. Sharon Blackie, *If Women Rose Rooted* (September Publishing, 2016), 94.

111. Sharon Blackie, *If Women Rose Rooted* (September Publishing, 2016), 336.

112. Jan L. Richardson, *In the Sanctuary of Women: A Companion for Reflection and Prayer* (Upper Room Books, 2010), 37.

113. Katty Kay and Claire Shipman, *The Confidence Code: The Science and Art of Self-Assurance—What Women Should Know* (HarperCollins, 2014), 133.

114. Wallace Immen, "How they managed to rise to the top," The Globe and Mail, Friday, Nov. 13, 2009; available from http://www.theglobeandmail.com/report-on-business/how-they-managed-to-rise-to-the-top/article1361762/; accessed April 27, 2010.

115. Jane Stephens and Stephan Zades, *Mad Dogs, Dreamers and Sages: Growth in the Age of Ideas* (Elounda Press, 2003), 92.

Chapter Twelve: Expanded Perspective and Influence

116. Rosabeth Moss Kanter, *Confidence: How Winning Streaks and Losing Streaks Begin and End* (Three Rivers Press, 2006), 8.

117. See Dr. Marilee Adams' work on this.

118. Anna Fels, *Necessary Dreams: Ambition in Women's Changing Lives* (Pantheon Books, 2004), xvii.

Bibliography

Bandura, A. *Self-Efficacy: The Exercise of Control*. W.H. Freeman, 1997.

Barsch, Joanna and Susie Cranston. *How Remarkable Women Lead*. Crown Business, 2011.

Blackie, Sharon. *If Women Rose Rooted: A Journey to Authenticity and Belonging*. September Publishing, 2017.

Belenky, Mary Field et al. *Women's Ways of Knowing: The Development of Self, Voice and Mind*, 10th ed. Basic Books, 1997.

Brown, Brené. *Braving the Wilderness*. Random House, 2017.

Buckingham, Marcus. *Find Your Strongest Life: What the Happiest and Most Successful Women Do Differently*. Thomas Nelson, 2009.

Coughlin, Linda, Ellen Wingard, Keith Hollihan eds. *Enlightened Power: How Women are Transforming the Practice of Leadership*. Jossey-Bass, 2005.

Clark, Taylor. *Starbucked: A Double-Tall Tale of Caffeine, Commerce, and Culture*. Back Bay Books, 2008.

Dweck, Carol. *Mindset: The New Psychology of Success*. Random House Digital, 2006.

Fels, Anna. *Necessary Dreams: Ambition in Women's Changing Lives*. Pantheon Books, 2004.

Heim, Pat and Susan A. Murphy, *In the Company of Women: Indirect Aggression Among Women, Why We Hurt Each Other and How to Stop*. Jeremy P. Tarcher/Putnam, Penguin, 2001.

Kanter, Rosabeth Moss. *Confidence: How Winning Streaks and Losing Streaks Begin and End*. Three Rivers Press, 2006.

Katty Kay and Claire Shipman. *The Confidence Code: The Science and Art of Self-Assurance—What Women Should Know*. HarperBusiness, 2014.

King, Thomas. *The Truth About Stories, A Native Narrative*. Anansi, 2003.

Kristof, Nicholas D. and Sheryl WuDunn. *Half the Sky: Turning Oppression into Opportunity for Women Worldwide*. Knopf, 2009.

Lederach, John Paul. *The Little Book of Conflict Transformation*. Good Books, 2003.

Martin, Courtney. *Perfect Girls, Starving Daughters*. Berkley, 2008.

Okri, Ben. *A Way of Being Free*. Orion, 1997.

Pattillo Beals, Melba. *I will not fear: My story of a lifetime of building faith under fire*. Baker, 2018.

Richardson, Jan L. *In the Sanctuary of Women: A Companion for Reflection and Prayer*. Upper Room Books, 2010.

Rukuni, Mandivamba. *Leading Afrika*. Penguin Books, 2009.

Simmons, Rachel. *Enough as She Is: How to Help Girls Move Beyond Impossible Standards of Success to Live Healthy, Happy, and Fulfilling Lives*. HarperCollins, 2018.

Tarr-Whelan, Linda. *Women Lead the Way: Your Guide to Stepping Up to Leadership and Changing the World.* Barrett-Koehler, 2009.

Wittenberg-Cox, Avivah & Alison Maitland. *Why Women Mean Business.* Wiley, 2009.

Zehr, Howard. *The Little Book of Restorative Justice.* Good Books, 2002.

CPSIA information can be obtained
at www.ICGtesting.com
Printed in the USA
BVHW061243080321
601998BV00010B/1055